SHOULD CHRISTIANS PROSPER

REVIEWS

Jim Hooks has written a timely book. After years of testing the principles of this work in seminar settings and seeing tremendous results he has now made the material available on a mass scale. His material is biblically based and very balanced. I recommend the reading and application of this material to your life. *"Should Christians Prosper"* is more than just a good title for this book. It is a question that is either avoided or often answered in ways that over promise. Jim has dared to address this question that is asked by many, and done so with honesty and biblical integrity.

Wayne Anderson

Praising the Lord for putting this book into my hands, I am seeing my (HIS) assets in a totally different light. Wonderfully drafted and an easy read for Christians and soon-to-be Christians alike, Jim Hooks leads you to an understanding of God's Word with a focus on His promises relating to tithing and giving. A thought-provoking and action-generating book for sure. Blessings, Jim, for this fine work."

Vivian A.Lebrun

Review of *Should Christians Prosper?* By Rev. James H. Hooks

Conceived in the cauldron of a difficult, if not impossible, financial situation, *Should Christians Prosper?* Is a must-read for every Christian who's serious about being a Christian. Rev. Hooks writes from in-the-trenches experience, describing how he went from deeply in debt to prosperous by following principles he studied—and put into practice—in God's Word. Backed by Scripture after Scripture, *Should Christians Prosper?* Teaches going beyond tithing, the importance of giving and having the right spirit in giving, who really owns what you have, and, most importantly, going to one's knees to seek God's will before moving forward with any plan of action. Down to earth, easy to understand, practical, thought-provoking, and life changing, *Should Christians Prosper?* Is a workbook on what God expects His children to do with what He's blessed them with.

> *Michele T. Huey*
> *Freelance writer,*
> *award-winning*
> *columnist, radio*
> *personality,*
> *teacher, and*
> *writing mentor*

Should Christians Prosper

If you are looking for a good book to read this year, I highly recommend *Should Christians Prosper.* This book, written by Rev. James Hooks, is inspiring and Bible based. It offers insight into what God says to us through His Word about prosperity and also why some miss out on all the wonderful blessings and gifts He intends for us as His children. In addition, Rev. Hooks will show you what you need to do to have a positive and successful walk in your Christian life as God intended. It insightfully addresses many of the questions we all ask ourselves. Get your copy today and begin to discover the blessings God has in store for you!

> *Rev. Bill Rudge*
> *Bill Rudge*
> *Ministeries*

SHOULD CHRISTIANS PROSPER?

Teacher/Student Study Book

James H. Hooks

authorHOUSE®

AuthorHouse™
1663 Liberty Drive
Bloomington, IN 47403
www.authorhouse.com
Phone: 1-800-839-8640

Published by AuthorHouse   12/20/2012

ISBN: 978-1-4772-8401-8 (sc)
ISBN: 978-1-4772-8400-1 (hc)
ISBN: 978-1-4772-8399-8 (e)

Table of Contents

Preface

HELLO. My name is James Hooks. As a bivocational minister, I have done interim pastorate work and pulpit supply, taught Sunday school, conducted seminars, and preached in churches and at youth conventions. My studies at the C.L. Lane Bible Institute in Transfer, Pennsylvania, started me on an intense Bible study that has lasted more than thirty years. I learned that in order to teach in a manner that will reach the general understanding of your students, you must study everything about your subject and know it so well that you can break it down and explain it in simplified terms that all listeners will understand.

With more than forty years of experience in the insurance industry, I currently have a fairly successful insurance business of my own. I was with one company for nineteen years, thirteen of which I spent in management. In 1984, I started my own agency. A friend from my prior company introduced me to another company, one that specialized in church property and liability insurance. This started me on a long journey that is not only my business but also a ministry. My father taught me some worthy principles early in life that I have applied in both vocations and which I will share with you.

But first we must understand that the entire Bible is the *Word of God*. Sister Lois Lane of the C.L. Lane Bible Institute used to say, "There was not a seed sown in soils of the Old Testament that has not come to full fruitage in the New, and there is not a flower that blooms in the New Testament whose seeds were not sewn in the soils of the Old."

I was born in a small town in Pennsylvania, the son of a coal miner and housewife. When my father passed away at the age of fifty from cancer, my mother had to go to work to support our family of six children.

My father taught us children the principle of hard work. When he would come home after a shift in the coal mines, he worked around the house, fixed his own vehicle, and did whatever needed to be done. Nothing was ever hired out; we had to learn to do things ourselves. We each got an allowance of five cents a week. We didn't have much and didn't miss what we didn't have. However, there was food on the table and a roof over our heads.

I remember in my teenage years we had a one-acre garden that we had to work, hoe, and weed by hand. (When we eventually got a fancy push cultivator, we thought we were in second heaven.) I did most of the work. My older brother, Harry, would shut himself in the car with the windows up until he was sweating. Then he would go to Mother and tell her that he'd had to do everything. At harvesttime I would load up the tomatoes, cucumbers, corn, and peppers on a wagon and take them around town to sell. This is how I raised money to buy my school clothes.

After graduation I passed the selling over to my younger brother Richard. One day, he took a wagonload of vegetables around town and returned in a very short period of time with a smile on his face. He said he had sold them all. We asked where the money was, and he gave us a strange look. He didn't know he needed to get money, he said. It was then I learned that if you are going to be a mentor, you had better be specific.

Another lesson my father taught me was on sacrificial giving.

We had only one car, so we hitchhiked to the nearest town, four miles away. One Wednesday, I asked my father for three dollars so I could go on a date—a dollar for gas and the rest for a meal. I didn't realize at the time but found out afterward that payday was Friday and my father had given me his last three dollars. My having a good time was more important to him than being two days without a dime.

I was married at the age of twenty-one and later became the father of two children. In my first marriage, I faced a mountain of bills and pending bankruptcy. After counseling, prayer, and anxiety, my wife and I decided to go our separate ways. Through these trying times I continued tithing to the church. I had to decide whether to declare bankruptcy or pay the bills and continue on what meager funds were left. I went to prayer. The Lord didn't speak to me in an audible voice, but His answer was as clear as if He had. He told me that I had made an agreement to pay my creditors back. I had used their money for my purpose. It wasn't their fault I was in the position in which I found myself. The Lord reminded me of a book I once read by Christian author Jack Hartman, *Trust God with Your Finances*. Jack, a businessman with twenty-six employees, had also faced bankruptcy. His wife asked him if she should reduce their tithe to help pay the bills. His answer was surprising. He said no, *increase* it. At a time when he needed funds the most, they increased the tithe. He has been prospering ever since. I remembered those words and applied them to my own situation. I eventually paid off all my creditors with interest.

For ministry purposes I moved to Punxsutawney, Pennsylvania, where I met Laverne. She was the answer to my every prayer for a mate. She was—and is— truly a gift from God. We decided to marry—a big decision because I was still paying back my creditors. I needed to let her know that she hadn't cut the prize bull from the herd. I had a home needing over seven thousand dollars in repairs before it went on the market. I took another eight thousand dollar loss to sell it. I was two years behind in paying my income taxes, and my checking account was frozen by the IRS. In addition, I had alimony to pay. Because of the divorce, I had lost my church income. "Do you still want to marry me?" I asked her. She said yes. We then had a decision to make together. I know the Bible says not to let the right hand know what the left is doing; however, this does not apply to husband and wife. Both need to know the financial situation and decisions related to them.

We were tithing our income, and I asked her what she thought. Should we stop our tithe and pay these creditors? If we did that, we could be caught up in two years. We decided together that instead of stopping our tithe, we would increase it. It was not God's fault that I was in this financial situation. Why should we make Him pay for it? It was at that time that God sent His financial blessings and multiplied our income to the point that we were able to tithe *and* pay off the creditors. God then laid on my heart that we weren't the only Christians going through financial crises. Others needed to know that God is true to His Word and that He always keeps His promises and won't be indebted to any of us. That is what led me to this study, which answers the question Christians ask when going through financial difficulties: *should Christians prosper?*

The reason I chose to share this journey with my readers is that I hope it will act as a sign post, pointing the way to Jesus as our source of true prosperity. It was when I took my eyes off working to supply my needs and instead put them on working to supply the needs of others that God's prosperity came into my life. We are not put on this earth to use the people and the world to supply our needs but rather to use ourselves to supply the needs of others. It was when God delivered Laverne and me out of severe debt that I realized this. I then realized that we could not be alone. If we were experiencing these difficulties in life, there had to be many more Christians with the same struggles.

Many Christians are struggling financially not because of choice but because of a lack of understanding of the application of God's Word in their lives. Everyone needs to hear this story. If God will do what He has done for us. They just need to know how to place themselves in a position for God's blessings to flow into and through their lives.

— James H. Hooks

Introduction

IN my travels, I've noticed that Christians and churches alike live far below the blessings God wishes them to have. I don't believe it is because of lack of desire but lack of understanding. This lack of understanding isn't due to low intelligence levels but instead is the result of the lack of knowledge to unlock those blessings. This knowledge is not found under a single topic or in one chapter of the Bible but is scattered throughout, in over 1,500 Scriptures dealing with the subject of finances and prosperity. This twelve-part study will bring those Scriptures to the surface of your mind in such a manner that you'll be able to remember them for the rest of your life. By receiving and applying these directions from God's Word, you will change forever your views on Christian prosperity. When you apply them to your life, you will see results you never dreamed possible, and you will know the answer to the question, *should Christians prosper?*

It's amazing, but the older I get and the more I study the Word, the more I realize what I don't know. God still reveals things to me I've never seen before. I believe that's because God reveals when the revelation is needed. For this subject, the time is now.

God led me on a three-and-a-half-year journey that included intense Bible study and research to find His answer to the question posed by this book. I spent another two and a half years putting together this answer in a simple, easy-to-follow, effective manner that makes the information easy to understand and retain.

This study can help individual Christians and families who are struggling, churches that are faltering, as well as individuals, families, and churches that are prospering. Wherever you are in your Christian walk, you will be brought to a higher level of growth and prosperity.

What I have to share with you through these sessions will cause you to look at the Word of God in a way you may never have before. One pastor who tithed for thirty-five years said he saw things through this study that he'd never seen before. Neither had he heard it presented in such an effective manner. This valuable information found a place in my heart. I have lived it and experienced firsthand what God can really do in your life if you believe His Word. I found that God can bless you in your failures and successes alike, when you are down in the valley as well as on the top of the mountain.

I'll share with you a personal experience that almost stopped me in my tracks halfway through this study. God brought me under such conviction that I felt unworthy to continue. I am a seasoned enough Christian to realize that when God brings conviction, He wants to do something in and with your life. So instead of quitting, I surrendered my fear and doubt and just took God at His Word. Doing so literally changed the lives of my wife, Laverne, and me.

If you are married, I highly recommend studying this topic with your spouse, especially if you want to apply the principles. My wife is my greatest supporter, encourager, and the best helpmate I could ever pray for. She has been with me in the valley and on top of the mountain. Through my conviction and with her support, we put to work in our lives the biblical principles I'll be sharing with you. God has brought blessings far above our imagination. Much more than I deserve. I'll pass that solution on to you, along with the same challenge we accepted. I am certain that God not only can but also will do the same for you. When you receive a blessing, so does your family, church, and all those around you.

There are twenty-five areas we'll address throughout this study. These are the areas with which we struggle within our daily walks. I've struggled with all of them. If you have dealt or are currently dealing with any of the following issues, your struggles are soon over. Help is on the way. I'll show you exactly what needs to be done through God's Word. The answers may not be what you would expect to hear, but they are from the truth of God's Word.

Can you relate to any of the following?

1. I am working, but why do I find it hard to make ends meet?
2. I am retired and living on a meager, limited income. Can God increase that?
3. Why do I have feelings of inferiority?
4. I have tried so hard to succeed. Why do I fail?I have a business. Why does God not bless it?
5. Why do I have too many bills left at the end of my money?
6. I want to give but just don't have enough to get by, let alone give more.
7. I feel that I am giving more than my share already.
8. I have gotten pleas in the mail, asking me to give to a ministry and telling me if I do, God will give me anything I want. Are these for real?
9. I feel that if I give, I should not expect to receive.
10. I am looking for concrete answers to my financial questions.
11. I can't seem to handle money.
12. I have a spending problem.
13. I have a saving problem.

14. I feel that God just wants me to be poor.
15. I feel that God wants me to suffer.
16. I feel that God is punishing me.
17. Am I too materialistic?
18. God must not love me because He is not blessing my finances.
19. I am angered because I have given to people in need and they did not respond in a like manner when I had needs.
20. I feel that I am being taken advantage of.
21. If I give any more, I'll be in the poorhouse.
22. I feel that in order to get ahead in this world, you have to lie, cheat, or steal.
23. I give more than many others in my church.
24. I am dependent on others (such as the government, an employer, the state, another person) for an income and am afraid of losing that income if I follow God's direction.
25. I am at a dead-end job and at the top of a low ladder. There is just no way I can get more income from my employer.

I am here to tell you that it is God's desire to deliver you from all of the above. Just give me twelve hours of your time and learn how God wants to bring happiness, prosperity, and joy to the rest of your years. May God richly bless you in your study of this all-important information for your Christian walk.

Power Verses to Memorize

I can do all things through Christ who strengthens me!

—Philippians 4:13

Greater is He who is in me, than he who is in the world.

—1 John 4:4

Young man, you are strong, the Word of God abides in you, and you have overcome the wicked one.

—1 John 2:14

For God has not given us the spirit of fear, but of power, and of love, and of a sound mind.

—2 Timothy 1:7

Every Word of God is pure; He is a shield unto them that put their trust in Him.

—Proverbs 30:5

Thanks be unto God who always causes us to triumph in Christ.

—2 Corinthians 2:14

There is no condemnation to those who are in Christ Jesus, who walk not after the flesh, but after the Spirit.

—Romans 8:1

All things work together for the good, to those who love God and are called according to His purpose.

—Romans 8:28

If God be for us, who can be against us?

—Romans 8:31

We are more than conquerors through Christ who loves us.

—Romans 8:37

Chapter 1: Who's in Control?

WE are living in a blame-game age. When something goes wrong, we want to blame it on someone or something—our past, the way we were brought up, our employers—anything but ourselves. We are even so bold as to blame God. We want to pass the blame in some other direction rather than accept it as ours. Blaming someone or something removes guilt from us. As long as we can pass the blame, we never have to deal with the problem, so things will never change. Problems do not mysteriously go away. If not dealt with, they will be there waiting for us when we get out of bed the next day. Our daily activities then revolve around our problems in life. It is not that we love the problem so much that we want to keep it around; we just never learned how to deal with it. In order to deal with it, we need to know our part in the blame game.

**What lies behind us and what lies before us
are tiny matters compared to what lies within us.**
—Ralph Waldo Emerson

You may not feel that you are on an equal playing field with the rest of the world. You may not have a natural talent or a brilliantly creative mind. You may not feel that you have a chance at a prosperous life when there are so many others more qualified. There was a program on TV many years ago titled *The Equalizer*. This was a mystery about a man who was dedicated to law and order. He was of average size and not the strongest person in the world, but he knew how to handle his gun and was very good at it. They called him "the Equalizer" because no matter the size or shape of the enemy, his gun and his knowledge of self-defense made him equal. Not only equal, it gave him the advantage.

Within every child is a potential for greatness.

We have an equalizer that places us on a level playing field with everyone else in the world. That equalizer is God. We are all created equal in His sight. It is up to us to develop our knowledge, talent, and skills to use these gifts effectively. Being that God is our equalizer and the Holy Spirit is our trainer, we need to look to Him as our source of authority. To obtain the promised results, obedience is required in developing those skills. We need to follow His instructions, which are outlined in His Word, in that development. As we read His instructions and practice His Word, we not only become equal to the rest of the world but we are also given an advantage by access to God Himself. *"If God is for us, who can be against us" (Rom. 8:31B)?* What we have or what we become in life depends upon how well we develop our skills in using the Equalizer to combat the enemies of our souls. So if you have ever felt inferior to others, remember this: within you is a potential for greatness.

This first chapter will really get you thinking. It will give you answers to some questions you may have been asking. It will also let you see things in a light in which perhaps you haven't seen it before. It will create some questions. As you move through each chapter, the total picture will become clearer. The answers may not be what you expect, but they will be directly from God's Word.

God Speaks

"The words of the LORD are pure words ... Like silver tried in a furnace of earth, Purified seven times. You shall keep them, O Lord, You shall preserve them from this generation forever" *(Ps. 12:6–7).*

If God

- is the creator of all that we can see and what we cannot see,
- is sinless and pure,
- formed man from the dust of the ground,
- set the sun and the moon in the heavens,
- created all that is living upon the earth,
- truly spoke all into existence in six days and rested on the seventh day, and
- is the author of truth,

we can then conclude that there is nothing God cannot do. However, God cannot go against His own Word and still be God. If He went against His own Word in just one area, He would be a lie, and the Bible would be like any other book—unreliable as the ultimate authority.

We should be able to go to God's Word and use it as the ultimate authority for settling any dispute of man and soul. Men have tried for centuries to challenge the Word of God and disprove its contents by proving discrepancies. In so doing, they have added more proof that the Bible, which was written by forty different authors over a period of 1,400 years, had to be inspired by one mind, a mind that has never been proven wrong—the mind of God.

Over the centuries, there has been significant proof that this Book is the infallible Word of God. Being that man could not prove the Word wrong and his intentions are vile, he has tried to change the words to mean something different than what God originally intended. Good translations change the words without changing the spiritual meaning. Whatever translation you use, make sure you do your research. Compare Scripture with Scripture by using *Strong's Concordance* to compare specific verses in the translation you want to use. The translation should withstand the test of truth of God's Word to be God's Word.

Remember, there is a way that seems right unto man, but the end is destruction (Prov. 14:12). Make sure the translation is the inspired Word of God. Accurate translations are simpler to read but don't water down the Word. Translations exist, however, that watered down the Word, changing the spiritual meaning to cause people to think they can serve God and go to heaven without changing their ways of life.

It is natural for man to think highly of himself, looking for a God that conforms to his lifestyle instead of man having to conform to the Word of God. Man often looks for a god to serve him instead of looking to serve God. If you are looking for a god to conform to your lifestyle, you are in the wrong book. On the other hand, if you are truly looking for the truth in biblical prosperity, read on. As we move farther into this first chapter, we need to know beyond a doubt that there is nothing man can do to change God's Word. Attempting to do so is like trying to mop up the ocean with a sponge. It cannot be done. Words themselves may be changed, but the Word of God itself will never change. The problem associated with the super knowledge mankind has been able to achieve is that some people actually believe they can change God. Their efforts are futile.

> *"And God said; Let us make man in our image, according to our likeness" (Gen. 1:26).*

Will every man remain pure and sinless because God created him that way? I have a brother who works in a coal mine. He gets up in the morning, takes a shower, puts on clean clothes, and heads down the road to work. When he comes out of the mine at the end of his shift, he has black coal dust all over him and looks like a large lump of coal with lips and eyes. Do you think he goes through life that way? If he gets in his car with coal dust all over him, what is the car going to look like? When he gets home, do you think he's going to get through the door?

When he comes out of the mine, he has to realize that he is dirty and cannot go home covered with coal dust. So he takes a shower to wash off the mine dirt. Now that he is clean once again, he can go home, knowing he'll be allowed entry into his own home.

Although we were created in the sinless image of our God, we cannot go through life without getting soiled with sin. If we somehow convince ourselves that we aren't dirty, if we don't even realize that we *are* dirty, we don't think we need to get cleansed. Wherever we go in life, though, we soil everything we come in contact with, such as our spouses, children, and people with whom we associate on a daily basis. We also deceive ourselves into thinking we can enter into the gates of heaven dirty and soiled. The only way we can enter the gates of heaven is to be washed clean of our sins.

Believing something does not make it so. Only believing God will bring it to pass.

"…[L]et them have dominion over the fish of the sea, over the birds of the air, and over every creeping thing that creeps on the earth" (Gen. 1:26).

Having dominion means being in charge. God put Adam in charge of the earth and every living thing on, in, and flying over it. The man, Adam, was the representative of mankind and God's children and the physical father of all humans on the earth for all generations.

23

God gave His spoken Word. He put man in charge. This means God cannot intervene or supersede in the affairs of man without the express permission of man. He can work in our lives or decisions only to the extent we allow Him. God will not force Himself on anyone, but He will work in our lives to the extent we ask Him to do so.

God doesn't work like the CEOs of a lot of corporations. A CEO is placed in charge, and then a board of directors is elected to tell him or her what to do, how to do it, and when to do it. The board of directors determines the vision of the company and how to reach that vision. They will also remove from power any CEO that doesn't obey the board. Reaching the goal or vision is not guaranteed. The board may make mistakes because, after all, they are just human. Who has to pay for the board's mistakes? The CEO is the one who gets blamed. So the real purpose of the CEO is to have someone to blame when things go wrong, when the desired goals aren't reached.

God works differently. God casts the vision, gives instructions on how to achieve those goals, and offers help in any area in which we need His help. He will go before us when we ask for help to overcome obstacles in our paths. If we follow God's vision and leadership through instructions from His Word, we are guaranteed to reach the goal. The only way we can miss the goal is to not follow God's Word.

So when God puts man in charge, he is free to make his own decisions and mistakes without interference from his Creator. God has also given us the assurance that any time we get in trouble we can ask God and He will help in any area we need. He knows from the beginning that we are going to mess up, and He knows what to do to make it right. However, we then have to decide whether to listen to God or continue doing things our way.

God doesn't force us to do it His way or make us go in His direction. However, He does remind us that we can never get to God's destination or complete His vision without following His Word. He allows us to mess up, go it alone if we want, even hate Him and despise His instruction, but He won't force us to go His way. There is a way that seems right to a man, but the end is destruction (Prov. 14:12). He loves us when we mess up, when we are so dirty that we cannot stand ourselves. He loves us too much to want us to remain that way.

He will strive to bring you back in line, but He won't force you. When God put us in charge of all living things, He put us in charge of the physical realm, what we can see, touch, taste, and smell. He expects us to do our best, and He will do the rest.

> *"Then God **blessed them**, and God said to them, be fruitful, and multiply, fill the earth, and subdue it: have dominion over the fish of the sea, over the birds of the air, and over every living thing that moves upon the earth ... Also to every beast of the earth, to every bird of the air, and to everything that creeps upon the earth, in which there is life, I **have given** every green herb for food: and it was so" (Gen. 1:28, 30; emphasis mine).*

When I was younger, I was not very good at English. That probably hasn't changed much. What I lack in expression of words, I have to make up with common sense. I do have enough common sense to know that "have given" is past tense. It's not present or future but past. We as Christians spend much of our prayer time with God, asking Him for things He has already given us. God really must be patient. He sometimes may wonder, *What do I have to do to get them to understand? Do I have to hit them over their heads with a brick?* You will hear the words *have given* throughout this book. Remember, we can take God at His Word. If it says *have given*, we just need to accept it. If we keep praying for what God has already given us, we do so only because we do not believe His Word. Do you see that when we pray that way, we doubt God's Word? If we doubt, we can never move any further in our walk or achieve what we pray for. We have already doubted God. Remember, God needs to say it only once for it to be true.

> *"And the LORD God formed man of the dust of the ground, and breathed into his nostrils the breath of life; and man became a living being" (Gen. 2:7).*

Dust just blows in the wind; it has no substance to hold it. It is dried-up dirt. When God placed dust and soul together, Adam became human, *hu* referring to the dirt and *man* referring to the soul. This was after God breathed into his nostrils the breath of life. It is from that breath of life that man became human, body and soul. When God made man in His own image, it certainly wasn't the physical image. There is no part of God that is dirt. He had to be referring to His spiritual image. God left what to do with that image to man.

Being that we are made from dirt, we have to wonder how important we or our prayers are. Prayer is a two-way communication with God. We pray and listen. We were made to listen to God twice as much as we talk to Him; otherwise, He would have given us two mouths and one ear.

The Fall

- Satan used a serpent, a living creature, to deceive Eve.
- Satan could not come as himself because he is spirit and God had given authority of earthly affairs to man. Satan could not override that authority.
- Satan used God's creation, over which man was in charge, to deceive man.
- When Adam disobeyed God and listened to the woman who was deceived by the serpent used by

Satan, man surrendered his spiritual authority to Satan. He also yielded his members and his God-given authority of the earth to Satan.

• God had to judge. Judgment began where sin began.

Satan has no control over God's anointed and those under God's protection. He had to get God's children to turn away from God themselves. He uses the same tactics today as he did with Adam and Eve. He used partial Scriptures in a devious way to get to Adam. Those tactics are still being used today—on us. Satan knows our weaknesses and our strengths. He uses our weaknesses to break us down or turn us away from following God's Word. Everyone has different weaknesses. That is the area of attack used to bring down the strong. Knowing this, we need to shore up our weak areas and increase our strengths, one of which is an unconditional and unquestionable belief in God's Word.

> *"And I will put enmity between you and the woman, and between your seed and her seed: He shall bruise your head, and you shall bruise his heel" (Gen. 3:15).*

God Passes Sentence

The origin of sin is the devil. There is no remedy for the curse God brought upon Satan. The ultimate outcome of sin is death. It is good for us to know that sin always has a penalty. We live in a carefree society that has been deceived into believing sin has no penalty. The devil and his angels know their destination. They know that God has spoken His Word and will not reverse it. God has prepared a place for Satan and his angels. A place of eternal torment. A place where there will be suffering in an eternal flame. A place where there will be no rest from agony. A place where there is no love and total darkness.

In a recent survey, pollster Ellison Research in Phoenix found that 87 percent of U.S. adults believe in the existence of sin. The poll, taken from 1,007 adults demographically representing the United States, has a plus or minus of 3.1 percent error. It found that people interpret sin from their own perspective instead of from God's. In other words, an individual decides what is and is not sin. Those polled had varying degrees of different types of sin. Yet 65 percent believe they are going to heaven, and only .05 percent believes they will go to hell. This shows that 34.05 percent believe we have no eternal destination and death is the end. This is an atheistic belief. To me, the results of this study indicate that most people believe there is no eternal punishment for sin.

> *"Fathers shall not be put to death for the children, nor shall children be put to death for their fathers: a person shall be put to death for his own sin" (Deut. 24:16).*

> *"Then when desire has conceived, it gives birth to sin; And sin, when it is finished, brings forth death" (James 1:15).*

The devil has deceived mankind into believing there is no such place of eternal torment and that God would never send anyone there. That is partially true. God will not send anyone there. God gives us a choice of where we want to go and shows us the way.

God has prepared a place for the Christian. A place of eternal happiness and peace. A place where we will receive all the good we have ever dreamed of. God has not entered into the heart of man what He has prepared for us in heaven, a place of eternal life (1 Cor. 2:9). God has prepared a place for us, so He prepares us for the place. I truly believe the reason it is not revealed to man is because if we know what He has in store for us in heaven, we won't want to spend another day on this old ball of dirt.

Since the beginning, there has been war between God and Satan for the heart of man. Both want man to follow willingly. This war is between good and evil. Being that man's fall was caused by man's weakness, he gravitates toward the natural and not the supernatural. It is easier to follow evil instead of good. We all know it is much easier to swim downstream instead of upstream. To follow evil is as natural as swimming downstream. It takes more effort to follow God's way. The easy way is the most popular and most traveled. It also brings emptiness, bitterness, and want.

> *"Enter ye by the narrow gate; for wide is the gate, and broad is the way, that leads to destruction, and there are many who go in by it" (Matt. 7:13).*

The Judgment

God begins judgment where sin began, with the serpent. The devil was degraded and cursed, detested, and abhorred by mankind, to be destroyed and ruined at last by the Redeemer (signified by the breaking of his head in Genesis 3:15). War was proclaimed between the seed of the woman and the seed of the serpent, between grace and corruption in the heart of mankind.

There is a story of a wise Indian chief who taught his young braves that every brave has two wolves fighting within. One is evil and one is good. One of the youngsters asked, "Which one wins?"

"The one you feed," the chief responded.

A battle for the heart and soul of every man is raging between God and Satan, love and hate, good and evil. We need to remember that the one that wins is the one we feed. Sometimes we want to serve God, but we find ourselves feeding the evil. We need to make a concentrated effort to feed the good. We do that by reading God's Word, hearing God's Word, speaking God's Word, and practicing God's Word.

> *"To the woman he said: I will greatly multiply your sorrow and your conception; in pain you shall bring forth children; and desire shall be for your husband, and* **he shall rule over you**" *(Gen. 3:16; emphasis mine).*

We'll never know how Eve would have conceived had it not been for the Fall. We can only imagine. Did God have a backup plan? No. God knows the past, present, and the future. He knew man was going to fall. He also knew what He would have to do to restore mankind to Him.

This is what makes the love of God so hard to understand: how He could have loved us so much that before creation He planned His own Son's death on the cross to bring us back into a right relationship with Him. That kind of love we will never be able to fathom.

God knew Adam was going to fall. Through Adam's sin, death was passed upon all mankind. Eating the fruit wasn't Adam's sin. Adam's sin was disobedience. When Adam disobeyed God, he made the decision to turn away from Him and believe a lie rather than the truth. We keep making the same mistake today.

Would Adam have made that decision if he had known what the punishment was going to be? Again the answer would have to be yes. Why? Adam was deceived into believing there is no punishment for sin. Here we are today, being deceived into believing there is no punishment for sin. We even hear teachings to the effect that a Christian can continually walk in sin with no eternal punishment.

Where there is no fear of God, there is no fear of sin. Man came from dust, and to dust he will return.

In proclaiming the punishment for Adam's sin (Gen. 3:14–19), God did not take away Adam's authority over the earth. Man was left to his own evil imagination. Left to himself, man will ultimately bring destruction to himself and those around him. In order for Adam to obey the serpent, he had to deny God's authority in his life. When he did so, he stepped out from under God's protection.

God knows that when men make decisions of their own without His divine direction, those decisions will be based upon selfish reasoning. Man will follow what comes naturally to him, and that is self-satisfaction. When we don't allow God into our lives to direct us, we will do whatever is necessary and sacrifice whomever we need to in order to satisfy our own selfish interests. Those self-serving interests will lay people, even loved ones, on the sacrificial altar. In later chapters we will go into a deeper explanation of why this self-destructive attitude prevails in man.

Remember King Saul

God provided judges, and God spoke to the judges. The judges, in turn, spoke to the people. God's will was brought about through the judges. Through them God fulfilled His promise to man to provide food, clothing, shelter, and protection. But the Israelites wanted a king like the rest of the world. God knew they wanted someone they could see to provide for them and give them the things they needed. These basic needs were those God had promised. (He clothed Adam and provided him with food and shelter.) These are basic provisions that God offers all his children. They did not trust God and rejected Him. Instead they wanted an earthly king to provide for their needs.

> *"[They] said to [Samuel], 'Look, you are old, and your sons do not walk in your ways. Now make us a king to judge us like all the nations' (1 Sam. 8:5).*

> *"And the LORD said to Samuel, "Heed the voice of the people in **all** that they say to you; for they have not rejected you, but they have rejected Me, that I should not rule over them" (1 Sam. 8:7 NKJV; emphasis mine).*

> *"And you will cry out in that day because of your king whom you have chosen for yourselves, **and the LORD will not hear you in that day**" (1 Sam. 8:18; emphasis mine.)*

Why did the Israelites make the decision they made? It seems as though they were being very selfish. We can look back and ask that question, thinking we would never do that. When we begin to think about it, though, perhaps we would do exactly that same thing. Why?

It's natural to center all or most of our thoughts on that which we can taste, touch, see, or smell because that is the substance of the physical world in which we live. It's what we work with every day to make a living. It takes effort to have faith in something we cannot see. Israel didn't have the advantage we do today. Jesus hadn't come yet. Yes, they had history of the Exodus and how God provided for them in the wilderness. The crossing the Red Sea, the quail, the manna, water from a rock, crossing the Jordan, astounding victories against powerful enemies—these were all miracles proving God's love for His children. It's only natural to think, *You did it for them, but would You do it for me, God?* Humans have short-term memories when it comes to everyday life. Worldly people judge their relationships with others on what others do for them.

What I mean by short-term memory is not that we forget what God has done for us, but instead we think God has left us and forgotten about us. When we don't see God working in our lives, we think we must have lost God's favor and that He doesn't love us anymore. Having faith in someone we cannot see is much harder than depending on what we can see. That is why we think in terms of our worldly surroundings. We would rather believe and follow man than God. The decision of whom we will follow is ours: God, who is never wrong and never fails, or man, who makes promises and knows he cannot keep them.

Following God when times get hard is not for wimps. It takes willpower and determination. It's an uphill road to walk. Yet that is exactly what God wants us to do. He wants us to follow His Word because we love and believe in Him. Hard times are merely temporary inconveniences for permanent improvements. We are making the same mistakes thousands of years later when we doubt God's Word, which says, "But my God shall supply all your need according to his riches in glory by Christ Jesus" (Phil. 4:19).

Today our politicians tell us to send them our money and they will supply all our needs according to *our riches*. In other words, you give me a portion of your riches, and I will take care of you. We are still turning away from God and following the ungodly who lie, distort, make shallow promises we know they cannot keep, and also persecute Christian values. We turn away from godly leaders and follow the leaders with the largest promises and trust them. We know they are lying, and still we believe them over our God.

When we follow those who are ungodly to take care of our needs, we lay aside our belief that it is God who takes care of us. Doing so lays our Christian values on the sacrificial altar of disbelief. It's the responsibility of God's people to place godly leadership in our churches, communities, states, and government. It is not an option but a command. We should choose leaders who are led by the Spirit to bring about godly principles for people to live by.

God will not force Himself into the affairs of man without man's express permission to do so. God can intervene in the affairs of man only in the areas that man gives Him the authority. Thus, our prayers are of the highest value. They contain the key to bringing about God's will in our lives and the lives of those for which we pray.

Restoration

> *"Then the LORD God said, 'Behold, the man has become as one of us, to know good and evil: And now, lest he put out his hand, and take also of the tree of life, and eat, and live forever'" (Gen. 3:22).*

- As soon as God pronounced judgment upon man, He made a remedy for restoration.
- Old Testament history shows that God did not intervene in the affairs of man until His people had relinquished their own power to Him.
- God talked to men of faith. The prophets spoke to the people.
- However, the curse was still upon man. God could not lift the curse because He had spoken.
- The only way the curse could be broken was for sin to be defeated in the flesh with the shedding of pure blood. Man's blood was not pure and neither was the blood of animals.

Life is a journey from the cradle to the grave. God knows that along the way we are going to stumble and fall. When we do, it's like walking through the forest when it's pitch dark. We don't know which way to go to get through the forest and come out safely on the other side. We meet many people along the way who direct us, but they don't know the way either. They are as lost as we are, yet they still give us direction because they think they know the way.

> *"Jesus said to him, 'I am the way, the truth and the life. No man comes to the Father except through me'"* *(John 14:6).*

> *"But if we walk in the light as He is in the light we have fellowship one with another, and the blood of Jesus Christ His Son cleanse us from all sins" (1 John 1:7).*

> *"God is light, and in Him is no darkness at all" (1 John 1:5b).*

There are those who say they know the way through life; however, there is only one who knows the way, and that is the One that made the forest and the path through it. There is only One who can offer true direction and light for the darkness. There is only One willing to die for our sins, and that One is Jesus.

God Speaks to Man

> *"And so it is written, the first man Adam became a living being. The last Adam became a life giving spirit" (1 Cor. 15:45).*

- God had to take the form of man to defeat Satan and his works in the flesh.

35

- God took on flesh so He could exercise His authority on behalf of mankind.

Up to this point Satan had the keys to hell. How? When Adam disobeyed God, God passed sentence that by the sin of one man, Adam, death passed upon all men. The outcome of sin is death.

> *"Therefore , just as through one man sin entered the world, and death through sin, and thus death spread to all men, because all sinned" (Rom. 5:12).*

> *"For the wages of sin is death, but the gift of God is eternal life in Christ Jesus our Lord" (Rom. 6:23).*

- Satan bruised Jesus's heel (Gen. 3:15) through Jesus's death.
- The Spirit broke Satan's head through Jesus's resurrection (1 Cor. 15:22–23).
- Jesus entered into the pits and took the keys of death and hell from Satan (Rev. 1:18).
- Jesus is the first fruit of the resurrection, and as He was resurrected, we will be also.
- At His ascension, Jesus took the throne and said that all power and authority in heaven and earth had been given to Him (Matt. 28:18).
- Satan no longer has power over the flesh or spirit that is surrendered to Jesus.

There is a popular saying: "The devil made me do it." Those who walk in sin do so because they love darkness and therefore sin. We choose to walk in sin. We choose the path we take in life; we choose our educations, vocations, and destinations. We willingly give ourselves and our power over to the works of the devil. That's because we allow the devil in us.

However, when a soul is surrendered to Jesus, the devil has absolutely no power. The devil is cast out, and our sins are purified by the shed blood of Jesus. Did the devil make Adam sin? Can the devil make you sin? The answer to both of those questions is no. We choose whom we will serve. The devil has no power over a child of God. However, he can influence our decisions and cause us to doubt the Lord. He offers us the sight of physical surroundings to attempt to lead us away from the works of the Lord. We will cover this more in later chapters.

> *"Then the sun was darkened, and the veil of the temple was torn in two" (Luke 23:45).*

- Man was given direct access to God, and the powers of Satan were broken.
- When we give ourselves to God, Satan has no power over us because we are no longer of the *curse* but of the *resurrection*. This also means that death has no power over us. John 11:26 says, "And whoever lives and believes in me will never die." Do you believe this?
- The body will return to dust, but the soul belongs to God and continues on.
- God has prepared a place for us, and so He prepares us for the place.

God can bless only areas of our life that we let Him.

God Speaks Through Man

- On the day of Pentecost, God came to dwell within

man. In doing so, God speaks through the willing host of man.

- Because man, to whom God has given rule over the earth and all things living upon it, has God living within, and because God has power over both the physical and the spiritual, man can now move beyond his physical realm.

- Man and God working together have no limitations except in the areas of our lives over which we do not let God have control. We are now walking on God's power and not our own.

God could have lived anywhere in the universe He wanted, but He chose to live in our hearts.

What a tremendous privilege and opportunity God has given us! To have God live within us and speak through us to bring His message to the world.

Not only did God choose to live in our hearts, but He doesn't force Himself in. He comes in only by invitation.

- He not only loves us, but He wants us to love Him.
- He not only wants to live in our hearts, but He wants us to want Him to live there.
- He not only wants to speak through us, but He wants us to want to speak His Word to the lost.
- He not only wants to live in us and speak through us, but He wants us to talk to Him and bring our requests to Him.
- He not only wants us to bring our requests, but His desire is to answer our requests.

He doesn't want to be our copilot and go with us everywhere we take Him. He wants to be our pilot and take us where He wants us to go and where we need to be. What do we do as copilots?

- Follow the pilot's flight plan
- Fix what breaks
- Get out and push in case of a major breakdown
- Rest when we are physically exhausted so we can be ready to take over on the order of the pilot
- Follow the orders of the pilot

What does God do as our pilot?

- Makes the flight plan
- Gives the orders for us to carry out
- Directs and shows us how to fix a problem
- Leads and asks us to follow
- Does most of the work so we can go places we'd never have the power and energy to go otherwise
- Wants us to perform on His power and not our own
- Gives the orders for us to carry out

Many Christians treat God as their copilot. We get up in the morning and give the Lord a laundry list of what we need this day. If He doesn't do all that we ask Him to do when we want it done, we get an "attitude." We stop praying, reading our Bibles, or even going to church. We are so bold sometimes that we tell Him how we want our prayers answered.

For the next thirty days, get up in the morning and ask the following of the Lord:

- "What can I do for You this day?"
- "To whom do You want me to witness?"
- "To whom do You want me to offer a word of encouragement?"

- "Who can I point in Your direction?"
- "Who can I introduce You to today?"

If we can pray this way, we are getting out of the driver's seat, putting Jesus there, and taking the position as the copilot.

The only limits of our achievements are the ones that we place upon ourselves.

Conclusion

In order to move on to the next chapter, we need to be certain of our place in the life God has given us. There are three beings that have a part in our everyday lives, one physical and two spiritual. If we believe there is a God and that He has an active part in our lives for good, then we must believe there is an opposing spiritual force that seeks to draw us away from God.

If we believe what we have just read in Genesis, we must then believe that we have a choice in how we are going to live on this earth and a choice in our final destinies. Many people go through life avoiding this decision by either putting it off or not choosing at all. By not making a choice, we actually choose the life of sin, with all its destructive power, which comes naturally to man by the sin of Adam. Not choosing is to remain in our now natural state of sin.

> *"Then when desire has conceived, it gives birth to sin: and sin, when it is full grown, brings forth death"* (James 1:15).

Let's take a look at the integral roles God and Satan play in our lives, as well as our parts in our lives.

God

God created us, loves us, and wants to provide for us things such as food, clothing, and shelter. God not only wants us to prosper but also plans for us to prosper. God has promised to give us His inheritance. God wants to give us a good, fruitful, and prosperous life. God's love for us is so strong that He sent His only Son, Jesus, as the sacrifice for our sin. God wants to give us a life of love, joy, peace, happiness, kindness, gentleness, goodness, and long-suffering. God wants to give us good things in this life and the gift of eternal life. He has prepared a place for us for when we leave this earth. That place is heaven, where there is perfect eternal happiness, peace, and love without pain, suffering, or tears. God wants to bring us out of darkness and into the light and for us to live in the light. He unites our relationships with our spouses and families. He wants to lift us up, encourage and comfort us in our hours of need. He offers victory. God is truth and is always truthful with us.

Satan

Satan hates us and seeks to destroy our lives with a promise of a better life than God can give. He wants to draw us away from God and into a life of misery, ungratefulness, and hatred while destroying our bodies. He draws us from the light of God to a life of darkness and destruction. Yes, he seeks to destroy both body and soul. He wants us to sell our souls to him at the price of eternal torment. He never tells the entire truth, only partial truths to lead us away from God by deceitful promises. He divides our relationships with our spouses and families. He teaches us to lie, cheat, and steal and attempts to make us believe that is the only way to succeed in life. He offers failure.

Our Part Is to Choose

After reading the above, we ask who would want to follow Satan. You're right. It doesn't make sense. Unfortunately, the majority of people choose that life. Why? Because of the following reasons:

- That lifestyle comes naturally to fallen man.
- It is seemingly the easiest lifestyle. I say "seemingly" because it is actually harder to live a life of misery than happiness.
- It is a downstream run that requires no effort.
- It is the broad way and the way most traveled.
- "All my friends are following that road."
- It is self-satisfying.
- It appeals to the me-first attitude.

Following God is not the natural state of man, and few travel it because it

- requires effort;
- is a not road for wimps;
- challenges our minds;
- requires us to live by faith, not by what is seen but what is unseen;
- requires us to love others and satisfy God; and
- appeals to using self to serve others.

Why Do We Have to Make a Choice?

> *"No man can serve two masters: for either he will hate the one, and love the other, or else he will be loyal to the one, and despise the other. You cannot serve God and mammon" (Matt. 6:24).*

> *"And if it seem evil to you to serve the LORD, choose yourselves this day whom you will serve; whether the*

*gods which your fathers served that were on the other side
of the river, or the gods of the Amorites, in whose land
ye dwell. But as for me and my house, we will serve the
LORD" (Josh. 24:15).*

We ask God, "Why do you let people in the world go hungry?"

His answer is, "I have given you charge and told you to feed
the hungry and mend the brokenhearted."

We ask, "Why do you let people go into eternity without
knowing salvation, without hearing the plan of salvation?"

His answer is, "I have given you charge to go into all the
world and preach the gospel to every creature, first in Jerusalem,
then Judea, and to the uttermost parts of the earth" (Matt.
28:19; Acts 1:8).

God has placed the destiny of
man in the hands of man.
It is up to each individual to decide
where he or she will spend eternity

He built us the house and gave us power, authority, and
resources to take care of it. He also offered His help in any
area we have a need. Chapter 1 of this book teaches us that
we are in control of our lives. Even though you may be where
you are today because someone else held your back or put
you there, staying there is your own decision. Your decision
determines your success or failure. The key is to eliminate the
blame and take responsibility for your own life. Yes, it up to
us who we will serve. Do we choose to be held back by our
ill feeling toward those who have harmed us, or do we move
forward to the future we really want? Do we choose to serve
our bondage or our freedom? As for me, I have chosen to serve
my freedom.

What are we doing with that authority?
That responsibility is in your hands.

Chapter I Action Project

1. There are many things wrong in this world that are destructive. *I will not blame them on God but on man, who made poor decisions.*

2. I can't change the entire world, but God has given me the choice to change the world around me.

3. I have the choice in every situation to make good or bad come from it. This week and every week I will choose to make good.

4. God has given me charge over what I can see, taste, touch, and feel (the physical realm). I choose God to intervene and empower me to change the spiritual realm.

Chapter 2: To Whom Does the Earth Belong?

If you marry a child of the devil, you will always have trouble with your father-in-law.

In the last chapter we learned who was in control of this earth and our lives upon it. We can assume that if there is evil everywhere, it is because we have chosen to follow evil ways. Some may misunderstand our part as stewards rather than owners. God did not give the earth to us; He put us in charge, making us stewards.

In this chapter, we will see how God made it clear who owns this earth, all that is in it, all that flies over it, all animal life, all living things, all silver and gold. The three aspects of ownership travel together like the three kings:

1. God's ownership
2. God's supply
3. God's protection

If we do not believe God owns all we see, how can we believe He will supply that which we don't see? Believing in only what we can see keeps God out of the equation. God tells us that the world of the unseen is greater than the world of the seen. To see beyond the physical surroundings requires spiritual eyesight. That is given by God.

Divine Ownership

> *"Now therefore, if ye will indeed obey my voice, and keep my covenant, then you shall be a special treasure to Me above all people; **for all the earth is mine**" (Exod.19:5a; emphasis mine).*

If we are to file claim to that which God wants us to have, *obedience is required.* We want God to give us what His Word promises to give; however, we may not read the entire context concerning the conditions of receiving what is God's. That condition is obedience. Obedience requires effort on our part. It does not come by natural means. It requires work and dedication. It requires a want–to. If you don't want to follow God, you cannot claim that which God intends for His children. We need not only to read His Word but also heed His Word.

God says He owns the earth. We read in the Scripture that Satan is the prince of the power of the air. It is misunderstood that Satan owns and controls the earth. God says differently: God owns the earth.

> *"In which you once walked according to the course of this world, according to the prince of the power of the air, the spirit who now works in the sons of disobedience, among whom we all once conducted ourselves in the works of the flesh, fulfilling the desires of the flesh and of the mind, and were by nature children of wrath, just as the others"(Eph. 2:2).*

Land Belongs to God

> *"The land shall not be sold permanently, **for the land is mine;** for you are strangers and sojourners with me"* *(Lev. 25:23; emphasis mine).*

We can buy up every piece of real estate we can afford, but when we leave this earth, it stays here. It is wise to have investments for retirement or emergencies as long as it doesn't interfere or take the place of our investment in the Kingdom. I will explain later.

> *"The earth is the LORD's, and all its fullness, the world, and those who dwell therein"* *(Ps. 24:1).*

In the passage above, the *fullness of the earth* means all that is in the earth, the *world*, all our surroundings; *they* means every human. When we walk down a path, street, or road, we are walking on God's ground. It belongs to Him. If it belongs to Him, then we are not owners but stewards. God has given the fullness of the earth and the world to us for our use and for His benefit. Knowing it belongs to God gives us a feeling of reverence, not to worship the ground but to realize that we are honored to have the privilege of using it. We need to honor His property with respect.

A few years ago my wife, Laverne, and I had the privilege to visit Prague and Vienna on a trip sponsored by a Christian company through which I sell church property and liability insurance. There was something that stood out vividly when we went down the streets and highways: there was absolutely no trash. Compare this to the city streets or country roads in our own United States, where volunteers go up and down the highways, picking up trash and bagging it for refuge trucks to haul away. I respect those who dedicate precious hours to filling up hundreds of bags, especially when a few weeks later there is trash everywhere again. I don't know about you, but when I see trash, it says a lot about the neighborhood. It is one that I would not want to be a part of. We see those people walking past the trash when a trash basket is just a few feet away.

Let me get back to the other countries. I am a curious person, so I asked our Austrian tour guide about the litter laws in the country and cities. She didn't know what I was talking about.

"There must be some pretty stiff fines for those who litter," I said. "Do they put you in jail until the fines are paid or what?"

She again said she didn't know what I was talking about. Then understanding dawned. "Are you asking why there is no trash along the streets and highways?"

"Yes," I said.

Her answer shocked me.

"We have no litter laws," she explained. "Our young are taught from a very young age to respect our country."

That was it, so simple but true. Then a vision of our countryside came to my mind once again. How disrespectful we are! We live in the greatest country in the world, the richest the world has ever seen. Yet at times it seems all we hear is complaints about how bad we have it. I have noticed for years an attitude in our young of gloom and doom for the future. We have failed our younger generation in not passing along a bright vision of the future. The Lord tells us that without vision, people perish. We have been given so much, yet we show our appreciation by trashing it. What a terrible testimony!

When I look to see what our children are being taught in our homes and schools, I see respect is not on the agenda. We need to learn to appreciate what God has given us and show appreciation by offering respect. Each one of us has an equal reasonability to take good care of God's land. We have been given so much and appreciate it so little. With a positive vision for the future, we will be called upon to build up and not tear down. To clean it, not trash it. Appreciation is something that needs to be taught and not offered as trial and error to find our own way. It is the elders' responsibility to be guideposts to show our younger generation the right road to travel.

I have been told it is not for me to impose my morals or ways on anyone else. People have to make up their own minds about what is right or wrong. However, it is not up to us to decide right or wrong. There is only one who has ever qualified to make that determination, and that is God himself. It is our responsibility to point in the direction of the Lord. "Train up a child in the way he should go: and when he is old, he will not depart from it" (Prov. 22:6). Everyone one doing what is right in his or her own eyes is just like it was in the time of Noah.

> *"And as it was in the days of Noah, so it will be in the days of the Son of man. They ate, they drank, they married wives, they were given in marriage, until the day that Noah entered the ark, and the flood came, and destroyed them all" (Luke 17:26–27).*

We need to remember that it is God's property. He has given it to us to use. We need to let Him know how much we appreciate it by keeping it clean. By not teaching respect, we are actually teaching disrespect. By not leading our young in the ways of God and eternal life, we are actually sending them down the road of destruction. If we don't teach discipline and respect of elders and those in authority over us, we are actually making solid plans to visit our young in prison cells when they get older.

A major part of that teaching is respect for self. If they have respect for themselves, they will have respect for others. So in agreement with the tour guide in Austria, I say it is something that they have to be taught from a very young age. If the school, parent, or church isn't teaching it, where are they going to learn it? I am under the firm conviction that the only reason we as a people do not teach our children to respect is because we are not respectful ourselves. If we raise a disrespectful generation, remember who taught them. Also remember that they are the teachers of our next generation. If we do not respect what God has already given us, we will never appreciate what we want, and we have no right to ask for another thing from the Lord. For this reason many prayers are not answered in a positive way. We need to learn respect, and we need to teach it. God says when we pray, we should come to Him with thanksgiving and let our requests be known. How can we be thankful if we do not respect what we've been given?

Not only land but also animal life belongs to God: *"For every beast of the forest is mine, and the cattle on a thousand hills" (Ps. 50:10).*

God Owns and Controls All Money

> *"The silver is mine, and the gold is mine, says the Lord of hosts" (Hag. 2:8).*

This raises a lot of eyebrows and creates issues such as the following:

- If God owns all the money, why doesn't He just give it to His children so we don't struggle? This is a legitimate question that will be answered later.
- When we work for a week and get paid, we like to consider the money as ours. We look to the source of money as our employer.
- When we get a Social Security check, we look to the government as the source of the money.
- When we save up for retirement through investments, we look to the source of those funds as ourselves and

our ability to accumulate through sacrifice and wise investments.

That is how we look at it. However, the Bible tells us that God owns all of it. If we do not recognize that, we will consider it ours and not be as willing to give to His causes. We need to use our spiritual eyes to see the real source. Once we realize that God is the source, we can look at our government, states, employers, or our own abilities of earning a living as merely distribution channels God uses to bless us and to operate His church on this earth. The channels cannot create money, only use, invest, and distribute it.

All Souls Belong to God

> *"Behold, **all souls are mine**; as the soul of the father, as well as the soul of the son is mine: the soul who sins shall die" (Ezek. 18:4; emphasis mine).*

Each of our souls belongs to God and is in His hands the disposition and the use of it. God says the soul that sins will die. However, one surrendered and living for the Lord shall never die.

> *"And whosoever lives and believes in me shall never die. Do you believe this?" (John 11:26).*

God Provides Us a Place to Live

> *"Do you thus deal the LORD, O foolish and unwise people? Is He not your Father who bought you? Has he not made you, and established you? ... When the most High divided their inheritance to the nations ..." (Deut. 32:6, 8a).*

51

The number of homeless is brought to the forefront of our thoughts today. As the church reaches out to find and provide them homes, it is God that is providing by placing on the hearts of His people to use His resources to finance these projects. There are many such projects springing up all over the country. Yes, the state attempts to help by providing relief and food stamps. While this provides some basic necessities, it is not a permanent place to live with respect. We need to look past these resources and see that it is God providing. He just uses different methods.

Is there anything left that doesn't belong to God? If God owns all, then we do not own anything. Home, land, furnishings, car, money, food all are God's. If God owns it and we have it, we are in trust of His property, which makes us stewards and not owners.

We must accept these facts before we move on. Here again, if we as parents have the "it's mine" attitude, what are we going to teach our children? One day, I watched two little girls playing. One had some toys. A visitor had stopped by, bringing the second little girl. The little visitor asked if she could have one of the other girl's toys so that she could play too. "No," the first girl said. "They're mine." Her parent didn't say a word.

Situations like these present parents with a tremendous opportunity to teach sharing what we have with those who don't have. Sharing does not mean that you lose a toy but that two can enjoy the same toy, giving it twice the value. However, if the parents have the same attitude of "it's mine," they will not correct the child. Their children go through life selfish, mean-spirited, and insensitive to the feelings and needs of others. There are parents, on the other hand, who correct their children and teach sharing. Through sharing, others can enjoy the benefit of that which God has blessed us.

Remember, our possessions are not ours to begin with; they belong to God. He wants to share His property with us because

He wants us to enjoy it. After all, that is why He created it. We show appreciation to God by sharing with others.

Now that we understand God owns all, we ask the following:

- How do we get it?
- Why do some have more than others?
- If we don't have as much as others, does that mean we are not as good or as important to God as they are?
- Does it mean God doesn't care as much for me?

Unforgiveness does a great deal more damage to the vessel in which it is stored than to the object on which it is poured. This statement may seem out of place here. However, harboring unforgiveness could impede what good things we might receive from God. We may say we have a perfect right to harbor thoughts of unforgiveness toward others who have hurt us or someone we love. While God doesn't ask us to forget all they've done, forgiving them frees us to move ahead and leaves them in the hands of God. (That is what we do when we forgive.) It is far worse for them to answer to the living God than to us. But when we harbor unforgiveness, it destroys our joy of living and affects how we treat those around us. So who are we damaging the most? Ourselves. God will remind us what He had to do to forgive for our sin against Him. When we compare what God had to forgive in us, it sure makes it so much easier to forgive others. I know that there are those who do not deserve forgiveness. Neither do we. We cannot change or answer for the actions of others; however, we do have to answer for our own actions. When we forgive, we are then released from the burden, and that opens a channel for God to work through. Forgiving others is not for the benefit of the person we forgive but rather for our own benefit. Forgiveness releases us from its bondage.

<u>Divine Supplies</u>

> *"I will lift up my eyes to the hills, from whence comes my help. My help comes from the LORD, Who made heaven and earth. He will not allow your foot to be moved: he who keeps you will not slumber"* *(Ps. 121:1–3).*

Be careful what you ask for; you might get it.

In the mid-1970s, before I became a minister, I was one of seven who met one week in a mobile home in Greenville, Pennsylvania. The next week there were fourteen. We quickly outgrew the mobile home. Down the road was a Christian family that owned a garage with a second floor apartment, which was being used as a chicken coop. The owner said we could use it for a church. We kicked the chickens out and put up wallboard and lay carpet. There was enough room for about fifty to fifty-five to worship. I was elected to the board of trustees. Since we didn't have a treasurer yet, I filled in. We didn't even have a moneybag to carry the money to the bank.

One Monday, I was given the church funds to deposit. Now, I had deposited my paycheck on the previous Friday, putting in enough to pay the bills. The rest went into my pocket for food and gas for the week. That Monday, not having a moneybag, I put the church money in my pocket and drove to the bank. On the way over I prayed for our new church and asked God to help me to give more. When I got to the bank, I deposited the money and picked up a bag for the church money for future weeks. I'd just walked in the door at home when the phone rang. It was the bank teller. She said the amount I'd deposited was more than what was on the deposit slip—quite a bit more. I reached in my pocket, and sure enough, I had put the church money in the same pocket where I'd kept cash for my week's expenses. She asked if I wanted her to leave it that way or if I wanted her to send me a refund. I started to tell her to send me the difference but then remembered the prayer I had prayed on the way to the bank: *Lord help me to give more.* I cannot remember a time when God answered a prayer as fast as on that day. He helped me to give more by reaching directly into my pocket and giving it to the church. I never prayed that prayer again! However, I did learn two valuable lessons: (1) when God lays a need on your heart, the best place to find the money is in your own pocket; and (2) be careful what you ask for because you might get it.

Somehow I made it through that week without dipping into the bill money. I don't know how, but God had given "my" money to the church and met all my needs to boot. The true supplier of our needs is God and not government, employer, state, stock market, or our own ability to earn a living. God never sleeps; He is on duty 24-7.

Though we have allegiance to the above, we need to give them respect in relation to God. They are only avenues— channels—that God uses to bring us blessings. We should not look to them as the source. Look past them and see God as the source, the hill from where our help comes.

We then should not depend upon where our checks come from as the source our income. Assume that you are working at a job and you are already at the top of the pay scale and have just enough to live on, paying your bills and buying groceries. I have people tell me that their employers will not pay them more because they just don't have it. There is no way they can get more money. Do you see what is happening? That person is limiting what God can provide by what their employer can provide. The same applies for those on Social Security or a limited income.

Think about that for a minute. Do you really think God depends upon your employer or government to distribute that with which He wants to bless His children? Does He need your employer or the government, or do they need Him? It is only when we train our spiritual eyes to look beyond and see God as the true supplier that we can possibly begin to receive that with which God wants to bless us. By looking to our employer and government as the source, we are leaving God out of the equation. Our own lack of belief keeps us from prospering.

> *"That you may be the sons of your Father in heaven: He makes his sun to rise on the evil and on the good, and sends rain on the just and on the unjust" (Matt. 5:45).*

God provides an equal supply to all to take advantage of and to use. How do we know the proper use of it?

You may not agree with this statement. You may be thinking that there are people born with silver spoons in their mouths and have so much more than you have. I promise you that before this study is completed, you will realize that these people you are referring to may be the poorest people on earth.

God has provided us with equal opportunities in His eyes. He has created for us this earth and all the resources that are in the earth. He teaches us how to use them. He provides the fruit of our labors. Remember, we can't compare material things that others have and feel that we have been somehow left out. God does not need a rich worldly father to leave you his fortune for you to prosper. As we proceed, this question will be answered thoroughly.

We Need to Follow Instructions

> *"Look at the birds of the air; for they neither sow nor reap, nor gather into barns; yet your heavenly Father feeds them. Are ye not of more value than they?" (Matt. 6:26).*

Being children of God gets us into heaven and His promise of food, clothing, and shelter here on earth. What we have from there depends upon how we exercise our faith.

> *"Are not two sparrows sold for a copper coin? And not one of them falls to the ground without your Father's will. But the very hairs of your head are all numbered. Do not Fear therefore, you are of more value than many sparrows"* (Matt. 10:29–31).

One sparrow said to the other, "These humans, why do they go about and worry so?" The other sparrow answered, "It must be because they don't have a heavenly Father to take care of them like we do."

We spend so much time worrying about what we don't have and where and when we're going to get it that we miss out on the daily blessings the Lord loads us with. Like the old adage, we can't see the forest for the trees.

A man built a house on a large hill from where he could see the beautiful forest in one direction and the sea in another. Every morning he would get up and sit on the patio with a cup of coffee and enjoy the beautiful scenery God had provided. He needed grass, so he planted some, along with a few bushes around his house to dress it up. Then he planted a small tree line across the edge of the property, thinking it would look a lot better. As time went on, the trees grew and eventually blocked the view of the valley below, limiting the beauty to only what was in his immediate surroundings. He literally couldn't see the forest for the trees. I don't know if that is where the saying comes from, but we do the same thing with our lives. We get involved with things that bog us down and fret about everything. The walls of worry with which we surround ourselves keep us from enjoying the beauty of the broader prospective life has to offer.

God gives every bird food, but He does not throw the food into the nest.

Most people want to have good things. They want a comfortable living, a roof over their heads, food on the table, and the ability to enjoy the good things in life. However, many want these things to be given to them.

> *"For even when we were with you, we commanded you this, if anyone will not work, neither shall he eat"* (2 Thess. 3:10).

We once attended a church in the country, and every Sunday about half an hour before the service a man came to us, said he was hungry, and asked for either food or money to buy some. We invited him to the service, but he always had an excuse. His wife was home ill, or he had to get home to take care of an emergency. He never did take time to come to church. It became obvious he was taking advantage of us. There were a lot of things that needed done at the church that volunteers did on their days off. We decided to give him the opportunity to work around the church, doing odd jobs to earn some money to buy his own food. A tradeoff, work for food. When we made the proposition to him, he—not surprisingly—had an excuse as to why he didn't have the time to do the work. Nor did he have the funds to buy gas for the car to get to the church. We told him we couldn't help him. He informed us that we were a church and if we were truly God's people, we were obligated to give him food. I looked him in the eye and referred him to the above verse, which states that if anyone would not work, neither should he or she eat. He never came back again.

We cannot become what we need to be by remaining what we are.

We all have dreams of improving ourselves and our lifestyles. We have dreams of being able to do what we want and go where we want without worry. Dreams are good. God says that without vision, people perish. However, just dreaming is not enough. In order to improve our lifestyles, we need to do something different than what we are doing now. We need to move off center. We somehow have ourselves fooled into believing that we can be at a better place in the future by simply praying about it and letting God deliver. Well, praying is good, but God wants us to put feet on our prayers. James 2:20 tells us that without works, faith is dead.

Faith is not just dreaming that God will fulfill our prayers. Faith is knowing it. We exercise faith when we get up from our prayers and move toward our goals and dream with God's guidance and direction. Otherwise, ten years from now we will be just where we are now. If nothing moves, nothing changes. If it won't move, push it. Progress comes from moving forward.

Divine Protection

> *"For the eyes of the LORD run to and fro throughout the whole earth, to show himself strong in the behalf of them whose heart is loyal to him" (2 Chron. 16:9a).*

We walk in God's strength, not our own. The Lord travels throughout the earth to show Himself strong on behalf of those whose hearts are perfect toward Him. Our responsibility is to have our hearts perfect toward Him.

We all want God's protection from our fears and our enemies; however, we want that protection without making our hearts perfect toward Him. You may say that nobody is perfect. But we know the One who is. Without Jesus, we cannot possibly experience perfection. He is perfect, and we operate on His perfection, not our own. Our hearts are the gauge moving forward toward perfection. It is a precondition to receiving.

> *"I sought the LORD, and He heard me, and delivered me from all my fears ... The angel of the LORD*

> *encamps all around those who fear him, and delivers them" (Ps. 34:4, 7).*

God protects those who fear Him from enemies from all sides. Read it again: seeking the Lord is a prerequisite of being delivered from all our fears. Everybody at one time or another has fear. We fear what is happening and what is going to happen. We fear our employers, the law, elevators, confined areas, spiders, mice, and snakes. A certain amount of fear is healthy. If we didn't fear snakes, we could be confronted with a poisonous one and get bitten. The lack of fear could kill us. However, some people fear so much that the fear controls their lives. They don't go places because of the fear of having an accident or experiencing something else bad. We need to understand that fear holds us back and faith moves us forward. God does not call us to walk by fear but to have faith. Fear is the opposite of faith. We cannot serve God by fear. We serve Him by faith. Faith moves mountains. Fear makes them.

> *"He shall cover thee with his feathers, and under his wings you shall take refuge; his truth shall be your shield and buckler ... For he shall give his angels charge over you, to keep you in all your ways" (Ps. 91:4, 11).*

Anyone who messes with a child of God has God to deal with. God will keep us in all our ways.

> *"As the mountains surround Jerusalem, so the LORD surrounds His people from this time forth and forever" (Ps.125:2).*

We need to understand how powerful just one angel is. God used one angel to destroy thousands of the enemies of Israel. God promises to surround you and me with His angels to protect us. Keeping in mind their power, if they are surrounding us, then there is no power on earth that can destroy them or keep them from protecting us.

You may be thinking that you have been going through some trying times, with one problem after another. People trying to destroy you, break you, and discredit you. Where is that protection? Good question, one that's natural to ask. We need to remember that God never lies. God never fails. When God says He will send angels to surround you, He is truthful in every way. If any darts and arrows that people shoot at you, attempting to destroy you, get through that hedge of protection, God had to let them through. If He lets them through, they get through not to kill you but to grow you. They get through to help you be an overcomer. They have to be for your good. So when you're confronted with a problem or an unpleasant situation, remember the only way we can experience victory is to go through the battle.

> *"And the angel of God, which went before the camp of Israel, removed and went behind them; and the pillar of the cloud went from before them and stood behind them: So it came between the camp of the Egyptians and the camp of Israel; Thus it was a cloud and darkness to the one, and it gave light by night to the other; so that the one did not come near the other all that night"* (Exod. 14:19–20).

Jesus was in that cloud. The cloud provided light for the children of Israel and darkness to the enemy. It guided God's children but caused their enemies to stumble. That cloud led the children of Israel out of bondage in Egypt to freedom in the promised land, the land of Canaan, a land flowing with milk and honey. However, to get to the promised land, they had to go through the wilderness, which was filled with obstacles. They had physical needs of food and water. They wandered for four decades before they were allowed into the promised land. During that time God fed them manna from on high, sent quail every evening, and preserved their clothing. The garments they had on their backs when they left Egypt did not wear out in forty years.

Yet there were those who, when confronted with the hardships, wanted to go back to Egypt, believing that was a better life. God always, always, always leads us to much greater things than we ever had in bondage. How soon they forgot how God had performed many miracles on their behalf, parting the Red Sea so they could escape the Egyptian army and then feeding them and bringing water from a rock.

That same cloud directs us today. It saved us from bondage to sin and leads us to the promised land, heaven. On the way, we'll encounter many obstacles and hardships. When confronted with obstacles, some of us, like the Israelites, have a tendency to look back and think the life of sin was better than dealing with these obstacles. How soon we forget the miracles God has performed—and is performing—in our lives! How He feeds us from His Word and by giving us the Bread of Life, His Son, Jesus, our manna from heaven. God provides us with food, clothing, and shelter. How soon how we forget how He changed our hearts from ones full of doubt, fear, and misery and transformed them into hearts filled with love, peace, and patience. God wants us to move forward, and He guides us that way. Faith moves us forward. Fear holds us back. God wants us looking to our final destination of the promised land called heaven. A land where there is no war, suffering, pain, tears, torment, or darkness but a land that is filled with perfect light, love, happiness, and the desires of our heart. What we have to gain by following Jesus is far greater that what we ever lost by leaving the world of sin behind.

"But not a hair on your head shall be lost" (Luke 21:18).

"These things I have spoken unto you, that in me you may have peace. In the world you will have tribulation: but be of good cheer; I have overcome the world" (John 16:33).

There is not a problem we face that God has not already visited. *Have overcome* is not present tense or future tense but past tense. It is already taken care of. We will have tribulation in the world, but God has already overcome the world. Wow, that is good news! That means that we can go about our daily activities with our heads held high and not be defeated.

Were you ever confronted by people who tell you everything wrong with everything? They live defeated lives and blame all their problems on someone or something (other than themselves, of course). They will never get anywhere because their vision of the future is blinded by pain of the past, which they hang on to and drag into the present. They let their hurts and fears govern their lives and thus live lives of despair. They claim they have Jesus but deny Him because they place themselves in shackles that keep them from moving forward. They live secluded and sheltered lives with few activities and few friends. They are miserable and don't realize that it's of their own doing. However, they are the first to blame others for adverse situations that confront them.

If we truly possess Jesus, we possess the peace that He promises us. He *has* overcome. Just accept that and let the shackles fall off as they did with Paul when he was jailed. It was the Lord who removes shackles that man cannot or will not remove. Fear and doubt are merely faith in the devil.

Where fear and doubt are present, there can be no faith in God. Where faith in God is present, there can be no fear or doubt.

As we have learned, there is a healthy fear. For example, we teach our children when they are very young not to touch a hot furnace because if they do, they will get burned. This is a healthy fear. I could give many other examples, and you could also. This is not the type of fear Scripture warns us about.

An unhealthy fear is when we fear the things that God has already told us in Scripture that He has conquered. For example, as Christians we need not fear the devil, for he is a defeated foe whose powers have been destroyed by Jesus's crucifixion and resurrection. If we are not to fear the devil, we are also not to fear any of the powers the devil exercises in the lives of man. If we don't have Christ in our hearts, we can only have fear. If we do have Christ, He dispels the fear because *"thou art with me"* (Ps. 23:4).

> *"And do not fear those who kill the body but cannot kill the soul: But rather fear him who is able to destroy both soul and body in hell"* (Matt. 10:28).

> *"For God has not given us a spirit of fear; but of power, and of love, and of a sound mind"* (2 Tim. 1:7).

To claim God's victory over our life situations, we must claim His victory over our fears.

It will always cost you more to say no to God than it will to say yes.

Summary

All the earth,
all that is in the earth,
all that is beneath the earth,
all the fowls of the air and the beasts of the field,
all silver and gold,
all humans,
all souls,
belong to whom?
GOD.

Key Points

- If God owns it, God distributes it. His inheritance is for His children, and we share in that inheritance with Jesus Christ.
- God distributes to each person according to our individual faith.
- He has given us the keys to prosperity not only in the life beyond the grave but also abundance in this life. According to our faith, let it be done unto us.
- God gave us control of our own destiny and prosperity.
- God sets no limits for us. How much we claim depends upon how we exercise our faith.

There are two old familiar sayings that keep us from moving forward toward a positive outcome and fulfillment of our dreams. They are as follows:

**People are great manufacturers.
Some make good, others make trouble,
and some just make excuses.**

**Anybody who brags about what
he is going to do tomorrow
probably did the same thing yesterday.**

Chapter 2 Action Project

1. This week I will recognize that God owns all, physical and spiritual.
2. This week I will recognize that if God owns all, then I own nothing, which makes me a steward of God's property.
3. This week I will recognize that it is God who provides for all my needs. It is He that provides my food, clothing, and shelter.
4. This week I will recognize that if I am in God's will, He will protect me from all my enemies.

Chapter 3: How to Be Successful Where You Are

As we go through life, we struggle with this idea of success. We have read with admiration books of successful people. We think, *If only I could be as successful! I would have the admiration of people I've been unsuccessfully trying to impress.* We can turn on the TV any time of the day or night and see infomercials showing someone, young or old, with a success story. When they explain how easy it is to make millions, it gets our adrenaline pumping. It's especially appealing when they advertise that you don't have to have any education, experience, or know-how. You don't have to know anything about the Internet and can succeed without it. All you need to do is send only $39.95 and you too will be able to achieve the same degree of success. Wow, $39.95 and I can make millions.

Who wouldn't want that bargain? You say yes, but ask yourself, "Is this all I would need to spend?" The answer is a resounding "Yes!" You get the information followed by a phone call from a supposedly successful person who asks how much you can invest. When you mention that you were told $39.95 was all the investment needed, you're told that you can succeed with only $39.95, but it would take you many more years to do so, and you would have to go through the school of hard knocks. "How much do you want to make per month?" you're asked. It's ironic, but the amount they ask you to invest is directly related to how much you want to make.

This investment gets you your very own marketing coach, who guarantees success. You're told if you invest $7,000, you will make much more than if you can invest only $2,500. You're "encouraged" (belittled) to make an added investment. Does anyone get the idea that I've been there? The answer is yes, and many times. These plans—schemes—all work in the exact same way: they make their millions by getting your thousands.

Why do we do fall for this time after time? Because by nature we want to have "the good life." They have painted the picture of the good life, and we set that picture in our minds. We follow their directions to the tee. About 5 percent find that same success. They have arrived. Or have they? For some it does work, but for many others it doesn't.

Most who achieve the pinnacle of success have to go through trial and error. They may fail many times before they actually attain their ultimate goals. When at last they could have any material thing they wish, all they find at the top is heartache and emptiness. If they have so much, why do they feel empty? To fill the void, they try dangerous sports, drugs, alcohol, and bodily abuse. They just end up destroying themselves and those they love in exchange for the love of things and money.

There are many others who do not achieve the same degree of success as their mentors and as a result feel like failures. This causes them to have an inferiority complex and a very low self-esteem. This in turn affects their relationships with their employers, pastors, spouses, children, and friends. They draw inward and may turn to other means to fill that void, such as drugs, alcohol, and bodily abuse. They also find themselves destroying those they love and for the same reason: the love of things and money. You don't have to have a lot of money and things to love them.

If the results are the same either way, you have to question why to even try? There is a third alternative—the easiest path to travel and the path most traveled: Do nothing. Don't even try. These folks go through life without any feeling of accomplishment, and like the other two described above, they feel empty. Which one of the above three, then, is correct? None of them. The answer that so many people go to most remote parts of world to find is found in this chapter. I encourage you to read with an open mind.

Nothing dies more quickly to a new idea than a closed mind.

"I beseech you therefore brethren, by the mercies of God, that you present your bodies a living sacrifice, holy acceptable to God, which is your reasonable service. And do not be conformed to this world, but be transformed by the renewing of your mind, that you may prove what is that good and acceptable and perfect will of God" *(Rom. 12:2).*

We are by nature a proud people and unwilling to surrender our will to the will of another, even to God. It is this pride that causes us to make the same mistakes over and over again expecting different results each time.

Why? Actually surrendering our complete will is something we have guarded against since we were able to start learning. Even as little children we were reluctant to surrender our will. When we came to the realization that we could not get our own way all the time, we surrendered to the will of our parents. The one with the stronger will overcomes. (Unfortunately, in many households today that is happening more with the children that have the stronger wills.) The parents cave in to temper tantrums, which results in rebellious children who will keep testing the limits of how loud they have to scream to get what they want. What is sad is that the parents give in even knowing what the children want is not good for them. They think it's better to let the children destroy themselves than correct them as God's Word tells us to do. God instructs us to train up a child and not to have the child train up the parent. These parents don't understand that in the process of learning and growing up, selfishness comes naturally. Caving in to the child's self-centered desires will feed the selfishness, and the child will grow up with an attitude of entitlement. When the parents are not there to give them what they demand, they will demand it from someone else.

My daughter once applied for a babysitting position. She answered a newspaper ad for a sitter for a young boy about four years old. The parent came to our house to see if my daughter was fit to watch her child. That was healthy. After all, you do want to make sure the one you choose to take care of your child is trustworthy. She asked my daughter what she thought about correcting children. My daughter said that if little Johnny was getting into things he shouldn't and would not listen, she would sit him on a chair.

"No, no! We don't correct Johnny," the mother said. "We let Johnny have the rule of the house. We let him get into the cupboards, take out, and play with what he wants."

Listen to her weirdly strange thinking: "By letting him get into what he wants at home," she continued, "when he goes to other people's homes, he won't want to do that." God help that child. I don't know what happened to little Johnny, but I am sure when he grew up, the parents were willing to visit him in a prison cell and wondered what happened.

> *"There is a way which seems right to a man, but its end is the way of death"* *(Prov. 14:12).*

The ways of carelessness, worldliness, and sensuality seem right to those who walk in them, but self-deceivers prove to be self-destroyers. As we grow up, the competition continues. It's not healthy to surrender your complete will to another person. If you go to a hypnotist, you place yourselves in his hands and surrender your will to him. That can be a dangerous trust. He can misuse that trust and use it against you for his own gain or even make you look like an idiot for the pleasure of others.

When we fall in love and get married, do we surrender our complete will to our mates? If we did so, we would not have a marriage of two but an unhealthy, dominating relationship. It is, however, healthy to surrender a portion of our will to our mates, and in return our mates do the same. The reason for that partial surrender is love. It's when neither spouse or both spouses refuse to surrender that friction occurs, and friction causes arguments, arguments cause separation, and separation causes divorce. (And you thought it was divorce that caused separation). If there is no surrender of will, there is no love. A marriage cannot survive in a healthy way where there is no surrender of will.

Yet surrendering our complete will is exactly what God asks us to do if we are ever to achieve any degree of true prosperity. Not surrendering our will to another person but to God. Making that surrender requires real love. If we do not love God, we will not trust Him. If we don't love or trust Him, we will not surrender our complete will to Him. Many have asked Jesus into their lives but have not surrendered completely. Withholding from God and refusing to surrender completely causes us to live lives of separation from Him, not ever receiving the blessings God has in store for those who trust Him completely.

We cannot become what we need to be by remaining what we are.

There are many misconceptions about Christian prosperity. Many scholars believe and teach that Christian prosperity was in the Old Testament and not the New Testament. In the

New Testament we have Jesus, who is a fulfillment of an Old Testament law. This is partially true; however, prosperity had nothing to do with the law. It is a basic principal that God has placed in His Word, and it cannot be changed. It is the principal of giving and receiving, the principal of putting Christ first in our lives, vocations, and our giving. What we give, He blesses and multiplies.

Misconceptions about Christian Prosperity

Christians prospered in the Old Testament but not in the New. Prosperity is not needed in the New Testament because we have it all with Jesus.

These statements sound humble, don't they? But they're not entirely true. It is true that when we have Jesus, we have all we need. We have all we need to achieve goals and blessings beyond our physical capabilities. Having Jesus in our hearts gets us to heaven and gives us eternal life. Achieving the blessing that God wishes us to have requires us to use the power of Jesus within us to achieve goals not possible without Him. Those achievements require complete surrender of our will to the will of Jesus. It is that surrender that gives us the courage to step out in faith with complete trust.

Money is evil.

The Bible doesn't say money is evil. It says that the *love* of money is where evil is found (see 1 Timothy 6:10). Listen, you don't have to have a lot of money to love it. There are people I know without a lot of money that love it. Their lives revolve around it. It's all they think of. It dominates their thinking daily. What we love most dominates our thoughts. The love of money is where evil is found.

Money draws Christians away from Christ.

If that's the case, you don't have a money problem; you have a spiritual problem. Take it to God before you move on.

Bad programming on television draws us away from Christ.

There are ministers who call TV evil and encourage their congregations to throw out their TVs. But when the television is thrown out, the evil still exists. That's because the evil was not the TV. It is in our own hearts. If our hearts change, so will the TV programming. We will choose programs reflecting the biblical worldview.

Money can't buy you happiness.

Neither can poverty. Many people feel that money can buy anything. It can buy any physical thing. Happiness, however, is not found in anything physical but can only come from the spiritual power of God living within.

It's not right to give and expect God to give back.

If this is true, then we should not take up another offering in the church or take another paycheck for our labors. Neither should we expect an answer to our prayers. It would also mean that God created money only for the nonbelievers. The only reason we have a right to expect something is if it is given by God. In His Word, God promises that if we exercise our faith, He will bring blessings into our lives that we could not have otherwise. It is not a sin but a joy to look toward with expectation, knowing that God always fulfills His promise. It is when we doubt that God will deliver on His promise that we live without expectation.

When we pray, we can expect an answer. Not because we are so great but because God is faithful in fulfilling His promise. We work at our vocations because our employers promise an hourly wage. Is it wrong then to expect a paycheck at the end of the week?

He who expects nothing will never be disappointed.

I have heard an employee or a person in the church say many times that too much is expected of them. Here's a suggestion that will solve that problem forever: *always expect more of yourself than others expect of you.*

Worldly Views vs. Godly Views

In the introduction to this section, I made statements about success. I stated that whether or not you achieve great financial wealth, the results are exactly the same: feelings of emptiness and failure. Now we are going to take a look at the reason for this.

Since we were children, the world has taught us about success and how to achieve it. When problems confront us as we work to achieve success as the world defines it, we rely on our own life experiences to handle them. If we lack that experience, we often look to someone else's methods and follow the guidance of someone who succeeded.

We learn from our teachers, from our employers, through our own experiences, or through the experiences of others. If they do not have Jesus living in their hearts, though they may be well meaning, the only direction they can give is worldly direction. Hence, in finding worldly success, we live a defeated life no matter how much we achieve.

Worldly ways and godly ways are opposing forces. Unfortunately the reason so many Christians do not achieve the blessing the Lord has for us is because they apply the worldly means of achievement instead of God's ways. They want to follow God; however, they just don't know how.

Outlined below is the difference between the worldly and the godly. Once we know the difference, we can then choose which road we are going to travel. Remember, God's blessings do not follow you down the worldly road. He asks you to follow His road. By doing so you will open up a life full of happiness, peace beyond all understanding, and prosperity you've never dreamed of.

Worldly Views

Is there anything wrong with the following items, which are often indicators of worldly success?

- Big home
- Fancy car
- Expensive jewelry
- Bigger toys
- Money the main focus in life
- Wanting name recognition
- Exalting self at the expense of others

With the exception of making money, the main focus of life, and exalting self at the expense of others, there's nothing wrong with the rest. They become wrong when they become the reason for our work and our existence. They become wrong when we place them before God. We are faced with decisions every day of either following God or the world. You choose a path with each decision. It is an ongoing process, not a one-time event.

> *"You shall have no other gods before me" (Exod. 20:3).*

Anything that you place before God becomes your master—that to which you are a slave. Can you be enslaved to your money? Yes. Can you be enslaved to your job? Yes. Can you be enslaved to material things? Yes. What we become enslaved to becomes our god. God cannot answer a prayer and bless us in an area that we've put before Him without going against His own Word. God will not go against His Word in order to answer a prayer that is conceived in doubt.

75

Worldly Motives

- Self-centeredness—take care of self-first
- Importance placed on things—buy for self-satisfaction
- "It's mine" attitude—things are more important than people
- Earning money the number one motive—the more you make, the more important you feel
- Limits set in our own minds—anything the mind can conceive, the body can achieve
- Eyes fixed on others to set and compare your own goals and standards
- Completion of goals dependent on any one or more external factors (where you live, the stock market, the job market, other people, such as your employer, the state, the government) so you can have someone or something else to blame for personal failure
- Conformity to other people's ideals and means of achievement

Conformity destroys a man's initiative and independence. If we are going to conform to anything, let it be Jesus.

If the world can achieve so much by believing in self and physical surroundings, which are limited, how much more shall Christians prosper by believing in God, who has absolutely no limits? There are those so intimidated by the success and possessions of others that they themselves don't believe they can achieve. This produces an inferiority complex and causes lack of initiative because they are comparing themselves to others. On the other hand, there are those who make the mistake of comparing themselves with those who have lower standards or are low achievers. This produces a superiority complex that makes them content with their own lives. Instead of owning up to the fact that the low achievers can do better, they use them as excuses for their own lack of accomplishment. Instead of finding someone who is more successful and striving to reach or surpass them, they look for someone who hasn't achieved as much as they have and settle for much less than they are capable of. That makes them feel better and removes the guilt. Many people drift through life with a so-and-so complex:

- I do my job better than so-and-so.
- I clean my house better than so-and-so.
- I do more in the church than so-and-so.
- I give more than so-and-so.
- I am healthier than so-and-so.
- I dress better than so-and-so.
- I'm glad I'm not like so-and-so.

In the preface to this book, I mentioned that I spent nineteen years with one insurance company, thirteen of which was in management. My responsibilities included hiring and training my own sales staff of ten. Some of them had more experience than me and the others I hired and trained. I looked up to those with more experience, but I learned from all of them. There is not a person on this earth from whom we cannot learn something. God brings people into our lives either to learn from or to teach.

I found myself working sixty to seventy hours per week, trying to keep the wolf from the door and trying to reach my income goals. In doing so, I compared my leadership abilities to other sales managers. I was satisfied as long as I was in the top 10 percent of the region. I felt content even though the results weren't enough to meet my own needs. Little did I know that the Lord did not want me to compare myself to others. Later on I'll explain to what the Lord does want us to compare ourselves.

Those who fall into the trap of comparing themselves with others actually limit themselves to the lifestyle or achievements of others, therefore missing out on a world full of blessings. Comparing ourselves to others is self-demeaning, as well as self-deceiving. Why do we have a tendency to do that? The reason is simple: it offers an excuse to fail and a reason to live in a comfort zone so we don't need to try harder or work harder. We become complacent. Instead of taking responsibility for our own actions, we use others as a standard of our own achievements. It becomes a habit as deadly as substance abuse. Those with this attitude will continually set low standards as a goal. Setting minimum standards and failing to achieve them may result in depression. If you are going to make a comparison, compare yourself to someone who has achieved all there is to achieve. There is only one with that qualification: Jesus.

Many people say they would like to have enough money to pay all their bills and not have to worry for the rest of their lives, so they consume their energy trying to get more money, not realizing that money brings with it some unwanted baggage— worry. In my younger years, I idolized movie stars who had reached the pinnacle of worldly success and had millions of dollars. *Boy*, I thought, *if I could only be a movie star.* I started to watch the TV program which featured a different movie star each week. Almost without exception those who had acquired such wealth were either coming out of or going into rehab for drugs or alcohol. While I applaud them for getting help and having the courage to place their faults out for the world to see, the question remains: why do they turn to such measures when they seem to have it all?

There can only be one reason. All the wealth in the world cannot satisfy the inward yearning for peace and happiness. Looking to the world to satisfy those needs is futile because you're always searching but never finding. They learned the hard way that money cannot buy inward peace and happiness. Perhaps this is why the Bible tells us that the love of money is the root of all evil.

The Unseen Truth

It is human nature to search for self-satisfaction, peace, and happiness.

Worldly success

- has absolutely nothing to do with true success;
- looks outward for inward satisfaction;
- ministers to self;
- changes only the outward appearance;
- cannot satisfy the deepest needs of the human heart; and
- uses people to acquire things.

When the pinnacle of worldly success is achieved, you still feel empty and continue to search for more, usually in the wrong places, always searching and never finding. Instead of filling the inward vacuum, worldly success creates a larger one. We spend our lives trying to get ahead.

All of us have gotten hurt by others at some time or another. Those hurts are sometimes deep-seated. Instead of being able to forget them and move on, we harbor ill feelings. The hurts fester, affecting our relationships, our work, our health, and even our faith. Harboring hurts is destructive. We attempt to overcome the hurt by thinking, *Someday I'm going to get even. Then I'll get rid of the hurt I feel.* When and if that time ever comes, it doesn't provide the expected satisfaction. As a matter of fact, now you have to watch over your shoulder for retribution from the one with whom you got even.

We need to keep in mind that the person who hurt you

probably doesn't even know how much pain he or she caused. If that's the case, the only person being hurt is you. Hanging on to your hurt only holds you back from enjoying life.

Perhaps that person truly did intend to hurt you. The reason people try to demean others is to make themselves feel better or to hold others back so they can catch up and perhaps get ahead. Either way, you lose. You aren't being defeated by others. You're defeating yourself.

My daughter, Sherrie, came home from school one day very upset. When I asked what the problem was, her face turned red with anger. "This girl in school keeps picking on me," she said. "Someday I'm going to get back at her. I can't wait!"

We held devotions in the morning before the kids went to school. I decided to make revenge the next day's topic, using the Scripture, "Vengeance is mine; I will repay, saith the Lord" (Rom. 12:19).

When we had finished and prayed, I asked her, "Sherrie, what did you learn about revenge and getting back at the girl that was picking on you?" She paused and then said, "You have to get even before you can get back." I just scratched my head.

You can't get ahead when you're trying to get even.

<u>Godly Views</u>

God-centered, not self-centered.

We all worship someone or something. When we were of the world, we worshiped self. When we came to Christ, we began to worship Him. Who or what we worship is in the center of our life, the focus around which everything revolves.

God owns all and entrusts us with His property.

If we are truly convinced that God owns all, we need to treat what we have as His and not ours. There is a battle within each of us: it's mine or its God's. Too many Christians go through life losing that battle. This is a chief prerequisite to God's prosperity. We must win this battle to realize the victory.

God—not employer, state, or economy—supplies all.

Before God can supply, we must acknowledge that all we have belongs to God and that God owns all. If we don't accept that concept, how we can expect God to supply that which we don't believe is His? God never changes. What we believe does not change the truth that God owns all. It is our individual belief that gives us the faith necessary to know that He will supply.

Action Plan

God is the source of authority; trust in His Word.

Do we use God as the source of authority, the final word in all life situations? Do we believe His Word is interpreted by the Holy Spirit, or do we use human authors to settle situations with which we are confronted? There is nothing wrong with using the experience of others as illustrations that can cause us to grow, but it is wrong when we replace them with the Bible as our source of authority.

Believe in God, not self.

Believing in self limits me to what self can do. Believing in God opens up an unlimited resource to reach beyond myself. When my belief is in what God can do through me, it changes things. It helps me to recognize that with God, I can move beyond my limits. If God has no limits, why do we all have different amounts, with a variety of lifestyles that range from very rich to very poor? Why does it appear that some people have talent and others don't? The answer lies in what Paul wrote in Philippians 4:13: "I can do all things through Christ who strengthens me." That is, I can do all things through Christ who strengthens me *except those things that I don't have the faith to believe.* The only limits we have are the ones we put on ourselves through unbelief.

Differentiate between vision and goals that come from God and those that come from yourself.

Many of us go through many frustrations because we get our goals and God's goals confused. We pray to God for a vision. We then have visionary things come into our minds of what we believe God is going to do through us. Visions that bring us to a higher plane in life, a life of leisure and fun. We then move toward that vision and find ourselves in a world of frustration. Eventually we realize that God is not working in our lives to make that vision come to pass. Nothing supernatural is happening.

The reason for this may be that the vision was conceived by our own selfish desires, which are blocking the vision God wants us to have. In order for us to receive of God, we must put self in the background and God in the foreground. Make His will the center of our thoughts. When we move toward where God is leading, it doesn't mean that all will be well. When God moves us toward a vision, there will be obstacles. Instead of confronting the obstacles, we have a tendency to change direction because we think the obstacles mean God isn't leading us. We find ourselves wandering in the wilderness. Remember this: God never gives us a vision that is free of obstacles. He called us to a place where there are obstacles He wants us to remove.

The lesson is that when you are attempting to find God's direction, you can expect obstacles. He doesn't want you to turn away from them but move toward them. This is the only way faith can be exercised. God will never remove an obstacle while you're sitting looking at it. You must move toward it. When you can't go any farther, just take another step. That step is where you will find God. It is only then that God will remove the obstacle or give you the power to get over, around, or under it.

Ministry extends outwardly, not inwardly, to others and not self, because energy moves outward.

Let's think about this. When we come to Jesus and invite Him into our lives, He comes into our hearts to live. The Comforter, the Holy Spirit, teaches us from there. We read and hear the Word, and it goes to our minds, where we analyze the information for distribution. When we believe what we take into our minds, it is transferred to our hearts and applied to our life situations. The information comes from within and is exerted outward to those in need.

Many go through life waiting for someone or something to move them toward the vision God has given them. (God didn't give the vision to others; He gave it to you.) In waiting for something external to happen, they miss out on the true mission purpose. They depended on something outward happening when they had the answer and power to accomplish it within them all along.

Make God number one, not self.

While God wants you to use your talent and abilities that have developed over the years, you are not to depend completely on yourself. If you do so, you cannot achieve anything more than what self can provide. You thus limit yourself to the natural and are unable to use the supernatural, which gives us the faith to move beyond and achieve much greater things.

Some people stay so far in the past that the future is gone before they get there.

The past can never change, but present and future change every day. God encourages us to draw on our past experiences to learn and grow and to use them as stepping stones, not hammocks. Remember the past but don't live there. If you live today in your past accomplishments or failures, they will be harmful to your present. We're given the present to live in. We can learn from our pasts and not let them rule the present. If our thoughts are dominated by the past, it will block the message God has for us today and hold us back from our future.

By willingly living in the past, we cannot proceed and grow; thus, everything remains the same. Unless we do something different, five, ten, fifty years from now we won't be any different than we are today. If we don't do anything different, we can't expect anything different. That is fine if you're content and happy with your present life. However, if you want something better and want to move toward the vision God has given you, you must leave the past and live in the present. You can then ask, "What can I do for You today, God?" With a clear communication channel for God to work through, you can expect growth to take place in your life.

Compare the Two

Worldly: *Attains a favorable result.*

Godly: *Results in peace beyond all understanding.*

Though favorable results can produce temporary satisfaction, they cannot give us a peace beyond all understanding. That comes only from God, not accomplishment.

Worldly: *Gain earthly wealth.*

Godly: *Share in God's inheritance both in heaven and on earth.*

God provides us with wealth for one reason: to share with others. If we gain wealth and use it all for ourselves, it will never fulfill the need in every soul for peace and happiness. God has created us so this can be accomplished only by sharing.

Worldly: *Spend money to make money.*

Godly: *Reap what you sow.*

Spending money to make money is essential to worldly success. The world has applied a godly principal to worldly success. Spending toward advertisement, for example, is sowing a seed. The goal is usually a better lifestyle. Keep in mind that the end of worldly success leaves us empty and unsatisfied.

God wants us to sow in His garden. Sowing in His garden is giving to His ministry. That is, the divine commission of going into the world to minister to others. Then it is God who brings the fruit, which in turn produces joy, peace in our hearts, and happiness in our souls that can come from only God. From this new fruit we get far more seeds to sow than from worldly fruit.

Worldly: *Follow someone who is successful and follow their instructions to the tee.*

Godly: *Follow the Lord through His Word and follow His directions.*

Following directions is essential to any success, worldly or godly. If you want to succeed, you certainly don't want to go to someone who has failed and ask for direction. You go to those who have already proven themselves to be successful. Success qualifies a person to direct others. You might ask who would go to someone who is unsuccessful to find success. The answer may shock you. People with negative attitudes spend their lives doing just that, without ever realizing what they are doing wrong.

In my early years in management with a large insurance company, I hired and trained new salespeople. Part of my interview process was to ask the applicants to go back home and think about their decision. This would offer them a chance to speak with someone else. When they came back in for a second interview, I would ask them who they spoke to and why. Some said their mothers, fathers, or someone else. Some said that they spoke to an insurance man that had left the business and went in another career direction. When I heard those answers, I immediately discontinued the interview. You see, whoever they spoke to would determine their level of success. If they spoke to someone who left the business, they weren't interested in succeeding. They were more worried about failing. Now, if the applicant spoke to a successful insurance person, I was interested.

Those who speak to those who have failed do not want to pay the price to succeed. A person who has failed can show them only how to fail. What other kind of answer can be expected? So it is with our Christian walk. If we want to be successful in our Christian walk, we need to go to someone who is successful in his or her Christian walk. Who better to go to than Jesus? He is the only one qualified to show us the way to eternal life, peace in our souls, and happiness. He owns all and controls all. Yet we go to the world to show us the way to success, which we define as having all the worldly things we desire to have. No matter how much the world achieves through the gaining of wealth, the end is misery and emptiness. No one wants misery and emptiness. Whether we realize it or not, we are following a program of failure by asking advice of someone who is failing. What we all want is peace in our souls, happiness in life, and eternal life, all which we cannot provide on our own or through the efforts of others. We need to look to the only One qualified to show us the way to that end: Jesus.

Worldly: *Follow the Japanese proverb, "Fall down six times; get up seven."*

Godly: *Strive for the mark, "You will prosper in due season if you do not faint."*

This Japanese proverb, like many other worldly success

principles, seems to be taken from the pages of the Bible. They are, however, applied by selfish means instead of godly, and they just appear to be successful. They have limitations of physical surroundings. Physical surroundings were all created by God.

When we apply godly principles to God's work, we are taken to heights beyond our powers or wildest dreams. Once we move beyond the physical, we are moving into the impossible. We are now working in the miracle realm. When we use words like *can't* or *impossible*, we demean God. We are placing our physical limits on God instead of placing God's limitless possibilities to our lives. With God, nothing is impossible.

> *"But Jesus looked at them and said unto them, with men this is impossible; but with God all things are possible" (Matt. 19:26).*

Worldly: *Learn by your own mistakes.*

Godly: *If you sin, you have an advocate with the Father. Ask forgiveness, and you will be forgiven.*

Everybody has made mistakes. Wise are the ones who learn by others' mistakes instead of their own. However, learning by your own mistakes makes you learn in such a way that you never forget. There are those who make mistakes that are immoral or illegal, and they pay the price. Every mistake carries its own price to pay. That price is unavoidable. Some people do illegal things and think they have gotten away with them because they have never gotten caught. Because they haven't been caught, the temptation is there to continue until they are. But payday eventually comes. They may get away with their wrongdoing in this world, but they will still have to answer to God.

Christians have that same type of thinking, but God can change that thinking through His Word (see Romans 12:2 and Philippians 4:8). Some learn by reading and heeding. Others have to learn by their own mistakes.

If we break man's law, we have to answer to man. If we sin against the Father, even though we know the consequence of sin is death, we are still tempted to do things we know the Lord warns us against. With our earthly justice system, we pay the penalty when we get caught, although some get away with breaking the law. With Jesus we get caught the instant we do wrong, and we can never get away with it. We can convince ourselves that we're getting away with it because we haven't yet received any punishment. Jesus is long-suffering and gives plenty of room for repentance. He wants us to recognize the wrong through conviction from the Holy Spirit and the written Word of God. Jesus has already paid the penalty of sin. When we repent, God's Word tells us the following:

> *"My little children, these things write I unto you, that ye sin not. And if any man sin, we have an advocate with the Father, Jesus Christ the righteous"* (1 John 2:1).

> *"If we confess our sins, He is faithful and just to forgive us our sins, and to cleanse us from all unrighteousness"* (1 John 1:9).

Worldly: *Ownership of all that you've obtained is yours.*

Godly: *Ownership of all that you have is God's, not yours.*

One of the hardest lessons to learn is that of ownership. While in the world, we work for a living, and we work hard for it. We earn and save money so we can have the things we desire, such as a nice home, car, and other things. We sign on the dotted line, stating that we own it. Or do we? If we purchase a home through a mortgage, we sign legal papers, so surely we must own it. We pay taxes on it, don't we? If we don't make the mortgage payments, though, the mortgage company or bank or whoever financed the mortgage will repossess "our" property. To whom did it really belong?

Let's use another illustration. Say we purchase the same home but do not mortgage it and don't pay the taxes on it. What happens then? The government will come and sell your house, and you can't do a thing about it. So, who really owns it?

Let's look at yet another illustration. We purchase the same house, make all payments, and pay all taxes. When we die, though, whoever inherits our property has to pay a "death" tax. Again, who really owns it?

Actually, the laws state that no matter how much you pay for property, the real owner of all land is the state. It has final distribution and ownership. Eventually all land will go back to the state, even upon death. If you do not have a will, the state will determine who will get your property, who will take possession. This means that no matter how much we work for it or pay for it, we never own it. We are merely stewards of the property for the state. We just have a right to use and profit by it until the state says differently.

In reality, though, the state doesn't own it either. God's law supersedes the laws of the state and is the higher law. He says, however, that while we live, we must obey the law of the land. We do need to look past the state and see God as the owner instead of the state or ourselves. Being stewards for God rather than the state holds us to a higher power. While Christians submit to a higher power, they can enjoy the benefits of that higher power. Those benefits are outlined in the Word of God.

Worldly: *You make more than you can spend.*

Godly: *You will receive abundance in this lifetime and the life beyond.*

Early in his career, Garth Brooks said that he'd already earned more than he could spend in his—and his children's—lifetimes.

I love country music and enjoy the music of Garth Brooks. It makes my heart sing when I see someone who has a story of coming from such hardships as he did develop and use their talent for the good. In so doing, they benefit themselves with the rewards. I enjoy seeing people honestly getting ahead. But no matter the extent of achievement, worldly success never fills the inner void and can never provide true peace and satisfaction. That comes only from God. I don't know where Garth stands with the Lord, but I'm sure he will be the first to tell you that all the excitement of worldly success cannot offer that type of satisfaction.

Worldly: *Believe in self and what I can do.*

Godly: *Believe in the Lord Jesus and what He can do through you.*

Believing in yourself is the first rule in worldly success. That is great as long as self will does not replace God's will. You can reach your goals believing in self but not achieve true success of satisfying that inter vacuum of having peace and happiness. Sometimes, however, that requires a sacrifice of family or loved ones or your own principles. If you don't believe in yourself, you cannot have any degree of success greater than how much you believe in yourself. All of us have shortcomings, imperfections that we see in ourselves that we know will hold us back. These may be lack of intelligence, memory, ability to learn, or physical limitations. No matter what our desire to succeed, we still have those limitations. There are many people who have overcome physical limitations and achieved outstanding worldly success that others only dream of.

On the other hand, when you believe in God, who has no limitations, you do not have to rely on your own abilities. The only limitations you will encounter are ones that you set in your own mind. Does God change them? No, it is up to you to let God remove them when we believe in God's Word strongly enough to stand on them. He will make our weakness His strength.

> *"And he said to me, my grace is sufficient for you: for My strength is made perfect in weakness. Therefore most gladly will I rather boast in my infirmities, that the power of Christ may rest upon me" (2 Cor. 12:9).*

You see, it isn't our own abilities or disabilities that decide success or failure but our belief in God. We may have been denied by the world because of our limited knowledge, appearances, or physical or mental handicaps, but our faith in Jesus places us on the same playing field as the smartest and best that man can offer. We have the same possibilities as those we feel are better and more qualified. When we believe in God, He causes us to believe in self, not by our own works but by our faith in Him.

Worldly: *Success is temporal.*

Godly: *Success is permanent.*

Any achievements obtained through worldly means and motives are only temporary, no matter how much you achieve. You work all your life to obtain things you believe will make you happy. When you leave this earth, you will not take anything of this world with you. It stays behind for your family to fight over, which causes division in households. It was divisive for them when you were living. However, when you die it gets more so.

Godly success, on the other hand, is permanent. Anything you achieve in the world soon will pass; only what you do for God will last. We will get into this more extensively in later chapters. In the meantime, I'll give you something to think about: you *can* take it with you. Now don't read ahead to find out how this can be. That will be revealed fully when the time comes.

> ***Worldly*:** *Wealth is measured by how much money you've made and accumulated.*
>
> ***Godly*:** *Wealth is measured by what you give and not what you have made.*

It is not what you get that counts but what you do with what you have. Give and it shall be given. How we measure wealth and how God measures are totally different. We measure by what we have obtained: the more we make, the more successful we are.

God measures by what we give: the more we give, the more wealth we have. You may be thinking that's impossible. But is it?

> ***Worldly*:** *Self-serving*
>
> ***Godly*:** *God-serving*

We go through all of life working to obtain. Obtain what? Things that serve ourselves. We convince ourselves we really need something we want when we really don't need it but merely want it to serve our own ego or satisfaction.

The Christian's focus should be on serving God. Many go through years of Christianity, living defeated lives because they just didn't get the message that the reason we are Christians is to serve God.

> ***Worldly*:** *Great achiever*
>
> ***Godly*:** *Great believer*

Is it what we achieve that determines our wealth or success or what we believe? We will answer that later. Keep reading.

> ***Worldly*:** *Give because you have.*
>
> ***Godly*:** *Have because you give.*

This is a concept that the world cannot understand and one that Christians find the most difficult to believe. If Christians truly believed this without a doubt, there would not be a financial shortage in any church.

The only difference between a rut and a grave is the timing.

Back before paved roads, vehicle wheels were very narrow and all roadways were dirt. When it rained, the road surface got soft, and it became hard to travel. After much traffic, and especially through the winter months, ruts developed. Even when the roadways dried, they were still difficult to travel on, as the ruts were unavoidable. It was hard on the tires and difficult to steer. So when you got down in a rut, you stayed there. It was much easier and required little effort. Signs were posted along the road: Choose your ruts carefully. You'll be in them for a long time.

Many of us travel the road of life in a rut. We attempt to get out and find that it requires much effort. If we do manage to climb out, we have to be careful or we'll slip back into it again. After several failed attempts, we give up. "Why try?" we say. "It's easier to stay in the rut." With that destructive attitude, we let the ruts control our lives and determine our destinations. When this happens, we never get ahead in anything life has to offer. We stay our ruts all our lives. At the end of every rut is a grave—a deeper rut and actually not on the road at all, for it is a destination, a place of residence. It is not life that deprives us of having good things; we deprive ourselves because of our own lack of initiative.

True Success

You can be successful where you are right now. *You don't have to have a lot of money to prosper.* When your view of success is based upon the amount of money that is earned, you're focused on an outcome that leads to disappointment. There are many people in low-paying positions that I know who are successful in business and in life.

When my son, Scott, was a junior in high school, he asked me, "Dad, do I have to go to college, or can I do what I want to do?" My answer to him is one I'm offering to you: "Whatever you do, do the best job possible and you won't have to look for a job. Employers are out there looking for you. Find something you love doing and make a living at it, and you will never have to work a day in your life." Many people with their goals on dollars find themselves in a vocation that they hate or just don't like. They put up with it because it is well paying. They don't enjoy their work and count every minute. When you don't enjoy your work, it affects your home, recreation, and family. If you had to live for years in this atmosphere, although you gained the world, would you consider yourself successful? If you're miserable, you're not successful.

Money is not a motivator. When we make it a motivator, we will never achieve success. Oh yes, you will be looked at by the world as a successful person, but inwardly you are a failure in life. Although the world sees a successful person as someone in business for themselves, having your own business is not a prerequisite for success. Just as we all have different spiritual gifts, we all have different physical and mental capabilities. These capabilities dictate if you will be in business for yourself.

There are many more employees than employers. There are also many employees who are more successful than there are employers who are successful. It is not my intention to be demeaning, but I just wish to illustrate that if you have a goal of being a janitor or a refuge collector, you can still be successful. Have you fallen into this false definition of success that has left you empty?

You don't have to own a lot of expensive items or an expensive home or drive a big car.

These material items are what the world looks at most to determine success; however, they are far from indicators of true success. Let's take a realistic look at the attitude that says in order to be successful you need a big home, fancy car, or expensive items you don't feel you will be happy until you obtain. This misguided goal causes many people to make the decision to have those things before their finances are ready for them. When they do make the purchase, they look at the prestige of ownership rather than what they can afford and stretch their ability to pay. They think the following thoughts:

- When I buy a car, I want a new one. If I buy a new one, I will work harder to make the payments.
- When I buy a house, I want a new one or one like new. I know it is a stretch, but I believe we can do it.
- I want to buy clothes or shoes because mine are out of style. I know we cannot afford it, but we will bite the bullet.

This is self-destructive thinking. These people find themselves not having enough money to enjoy life. They have to squeeze their funds in areas of life that are the true reasons why we work to begin with, and they sacrifice inner peace and happiness. We are so used to making excuses for unhappiness and lack of ability to meet our needs that we even make excuses to God. We find ourselves saying, "God, you understand why I cannot pay my tithe. Scripture says we should pay all our creditors." We use God's own Word against God as an excuse why we don't trust or believe in His Word. Do we really believe God will fall for this kind of disbelief? This materialistic attitude causes division in households, in relationships with our spouses and families, and even with our God.

Have you fallen into this trap of thinking success is associated with having expensive material things? Have you found that you have obtained money and expensive things and left your peace and happiness tank empty? You have been looking in all the wrong places. You have been looking outward, for people, things, ideas, or success to bring you inner peace and happiness. But you've learned that places, things, your business, your spouse, not even your pastor can bring you this outcome that all of us desire.

Success/prosperity is not found in outward achievement but an inward experience.

We spend our lives searching the world for something that is found within us. If God is love, the only way we can ever experience true love is to have God living within us.

> *"He that does not love does not know God; for God is love" (1 John 4:8).*

> *"And the peace of God, which surpasses all understanding, will guard your hearts and minds through Christ Jesus" (Phil. 4:7).*

Success/prosperity is not having what you want but wanting what you have.

So many Christians fall into the trap of keeping up with the Joneses, wanting things just because someone else has it. Even though we have an item they have, when they get a newer style, we want the same. So we make excuses that what we have is inadequate, old, or out of style. Instead of appreciating what God has already given us, we complain. "I'm getting tired of trying to keep up with the neighbors," I told my wife in jest one day. "Let's just drag them down to our level." I said it jokingly, but too often it's true for many of us.

Remember the children of Israel who were worried about starving or dying of thirst in the wilderness? God provided them with manna every morning except the Sabbath and quail every evening and caused water to gush from a rock. Instead of being thankful, they complained. Be careful about judging them as ungrateful. Take a good look at your own life. Do you appreciate what God has given you? Or do you find yourself complaining to Him of your dissatisfaction and asking for something else? We will deal with this in a later chapter.

If you want what you have, what you want will look for you.

The only way we can truly want what we have is to want what God wants for us and not necessarily what we want for ourselves. The closer my walk with the Lord, the more I realize I really don't have the final answers on what is best for me or my family. Faith gives us the undeniable understanding that God knows exactly what is best for us, what does and what does not make us happy, and what will and will not lead us to a prosperous life. Jesus gives us a peace beyond all understanding

We don't need the sand Jesus walked on. We need the Jesus that walked on the sand.

There are many who have the opportunity to visit Israel to walk in places where Jesus walked, even if His original footsteps are layers deeper than where they walk. But many people don't have, and will ever have, the means to go. They may feel they've lost out on something.

Even though I desire to go to Israel someday, it doesn't bother me that I have not yet gone. We can go to Israel to walk where Jesus walked and be lost for eternity. It is much more important to have the Jesus that made those steps live within your heart. Then He walks with you in your footsteps. That is His desire—that you accept the sacrifice He has made and accept Him as the only sacrifice for your sins, the only way to God and eternal life.

If you don't have Jesus in your heart as the Savior and Lord of your life, take time right now to pray and ask God to forgive you for your sin and invite Jesus into your heart. Remember, God can live anywhere in the universe He wants. He chose instead to make His home in your heart. Without praying this prayer, it is impossible to please God. The world system of prosperity puts these ahead of God: money, success, possessions, and ego recognition. God wants us to prosper but only if things do not take His place as first place in our lives.

> *"If any man will come after me, let him deny himself, and take up his cross daily, and follow me" (Luke 9:23).*

Don't consume all your tomorrows feeding on your yesterdays.

God has given us our yesterdays to grow from and use as a stepping stone and not a hammock. By living in yesterday, we waste our todays.

Summary

When we make the transformation mentioned in Romans 12:2, which tells us not to be conformed to this world but to be transformed by the renewing of our minds, we realize that every future event or destination we plan starts in our minds. The transformation that must take place is that instead of looking outward to the world or other people as the means of supplying our needs and desires or life dreams, we look internally. We recognize that all that we have is given by God, and we show appreciation for what we have already been given. Then we are in a position to use what we have already been given no matter what we have and use our knowledge, gifts, and talents to meet the needs of the world and others.

This is the calling of every Christian. When we have made

this transformation, the Lord has a prepared heart with which he can work. He brings us peace and happiness beyond our understanding. (Isn't peace and happiness what we all have been searching for?) When we have achieved that, we have succeeded in fulfilling life's needs. Then and only then can we have the mindset to use our peace, happiness, talents, and abilities to help others get the same. When we are in the process of doing that, we are fulfilling the laws of Christ, which are a command to every Christian. *Go into all the world and preach the gospel, first in Jerusalem and then Judea and the outer most parts of the world.* Achieving that transformation is true success and the beginning of prosperity.

Chapter 3 Action Project

Ask yourself the following:

1. Do I place God ahead of each member of my family?
2. Is God more important to me than my friends?
3. Do I spend more time seeking God each day than I do watching TV or enjoying hobbies?
4. Is God more important to me than any possession I have?
5. Is seeking God on a daily basis more important to me than seeking financial prosperity?
6. Do I really believe God's Word?
7. Do I really believe God can do what He says He will do?
8. Do I really believe God *will* do what He says He will do?
9. Do I really believe God's Word applies to me?
10. Will I trust God in the areas in my life in which I have the greatest needs?

Chapter 4: Instructions from God's Word

Don't grumble because you don't have what you want.
Be thankful you don't get what you deserve.

BECAUSE of our sin, we are worthy of death. Sin separates us from God, and when sin is finished, it brings death. The gift of God is eternal life through Jesus Christ our Lord (Rom. 6:23). If God never gives us another thing, He has already given us more than we deserve. If we can keep focused on this when serving God and praying for needs, we will see many more blessings come into our lives that we would not have had otherwise.

Our God is not a God that sits on His throne, looking for ways to punish us for the wrong we do. Just the opposite! He is instead looking for ways to bless us and give us our inheritance. He is saying, "Please put yourself in a position so that I can bless you. I will release to you blessings when you exercise your faith. The extent of the blessings is in direct proportion to the amount of faith you exercise."

Too many Christians feel that by praying for something and believing that God will do it, we have done our part. That is not exercising faith but asking God to do all the work. That is passive faith, which doesn't require anything else except praying and believing. Belief is proven, however, when we get up from our knees and, knowing without a doubt that God answered our prayers, move forward.

Here is a dilemma in which many of us find ourselves. I once closed a service asking for anyone who wanted prayer for healing to come forward. A gentleman who was receiving disability benefits from Social Security for heart problems responded. I asked those of faith to come forward and pray without doubt that God would provide healing. A few of the very faithful came to pray. When the gentleman rose from his feet, he testified that God had healed him. The very next day he had to go to the Social Security Administration review board to prove that he was still sick so he could continue to receive benefits. He had a decision to make: claim God's healing or prove that he was still sick. His decision is why his name will remain anonymous. What would you do in this situation? Faith in God requires you to step into the unknown knowing that God has answered your prayer.

The same may occur when we pray for healing, get up from the altar, and still have the symptoms as before the prayer. Do we see healing, or do we see the symptoms and doubt healing? Faith believes God and that which we don't or can't see. Doubt believes only what we see. If we are to receive the good things God has in store for us, we must move past what we can see and see that which God promises. Could this be the very reason why so many of us live so far beneath the blessings God has for us?

Limits We Place on Ourselves

An experiment was conducted at the Pennsylvania State University in which a pike fish was placed in an aquarium. A piece of Plexiglas was then used as a divider. A minnow was placed on the other side. Now, we all know how pike love minnows. The pike was not fed. The hungry fish could see the minnow but not the Plexiglas. It headed for the minnow but hit the Plexiglas. This hurt its nose. The more it tried to get to the minnow, the more its nose hurt. Before long, it associated attempting to get the minnow with pain and stopped trying. At that point, the Plexiglas was removed, and the minnow swam all around the pike—unharmed. All the pike needed to do was make one pass and it could have had a meal because the obstacle that was causing the pain had been removed. But in the pike's mind, the minnow was not obtainable.

We all have set limits in our minds as to what we can do or what God can do through us. Because of these limits, we believe certain things or achievements are unattainable. We associate them with the pain we experience in trying to obtain them. When the obstacles are removed and we can just reach out and grab them, we think it can't be done and thus stop trying.

We create limits when we encounter problems that we feel we cannot overcome. We can never get beyond those limits until we make up our minds that we are going to overcome the problem associated with them. If God allows them, they must be for our benefit. We create limits because of our carnal thinking, which can see only the physical and not beyond. Only God can empower us to move beyond the physical limits. We need to understand that God doesn't place limits upon us but removes limits from us. Remember what Paul told the Philippians: *"I can do all things through Christ who strengthens me" (Phil. 4:13).*

Problems exist for our benefit, but our first inclination is to look at them as a negative and think about how they can harm us or prevent us from doing what we want to do. We can do one of the following:

1. Look at the problem as a negative. By doing this we are slaves to our problems. The problem creates a

negative effect on our lives and wins. We find our daily activities guided by the problem.

2. Look at the problem as a positive. The problem is our slave, creating a positive effect and working for us. We win.

We need to learn to apply God's laws to our problems, which will turn them from negatives to positives. Remember, no problem is too big for God.

How? If we ignore the problem and pretend it does not exist or that it will go away, we are relying on false hope. We may walk away from it, but when we do, the problem still exists and is waiting to come at us again. The problem must be confronted. When we confront it, we walk toward it to find the solution. The seed to solution is found within the problem itself. So we look within the problem itself for that seed. When we find it, we need to realize that it is a seed growing to bear fruit. The fruit is a blessing to us. Thus the problem exists for our benefit and not to our detriment.

Years ago when I was in management with a large life insurance company, I had meetings with my sales representatives once a week for an hour. One sales representative was always negative. Whatever the topic, he would look at the negative side. I had practiced and taught that there were two sides to every problem or situation, a positive and negative. As we have seen above, it is not the situation that controls a positive or negative effect but the decision we make as to how we are going to let the situation affect our lives and the way we handle the problem. This gentleman said you couldn't look at every situation positively. I asked for an example.

"What if you are traveling down the highway and come around a bend and see that an accident just happened," he said. "A car was demolished, a baby is severely injured, the father lost his life, and the mother permanently injured. What possibly could I find positive about that drastic accident?"

"I could have been coming around that bend two minutes earlier," I said. "That could have been me lying there."

At that time he looked at me as if he wished it had been. Remember the following:

- The negative always brings us backward, and positive always moves us forward.
- Doubt always causes us to go backward, and faith always moves us forward.

Which way are you going?

Nobody would have ever crossed the ocean if they could have gotten off the boat during a storm.

The True God

A man started out through a forest so thickly covered with trees that one day he could not see the sun or sky. After traveling for a long time, he knew it was nearing nighttime, so he started for what he thought was home. He was so certain that his direction was right that he did not look at his compass. But when he did look at it, he was surprised to find that he was going west when he thought he was going east. He was so sure he was right that he started to throw his compass away. Then he thought, You have never told me an untruth, and I'll trust you now. He followed the compass and came out right. We too have a compass that will never tell us an untruth. It is God's Word the Bible. If we always follow it, we will be safe, even though we think we are right. If it tells us something different, then let us follow what it says, for that is the only safe thing.

("Sermon Illustrations," *Gospel Herald* http://elbourne.org/sermons/index.mv?illustration+3492)

Wisdom vs. Knowledge

Knowledge in itself is useless to you, the world, or to God. What makes knowledge valuable is knowing how to use it for God's purpose. Wisdom is putting that knowledge to use. Wisdom can be abused, or it can be used. We abuse it by not using it or using it for selfish gain. There is nothing worse than having something and not using it. This is another law that God places in all areas of life, physical and spiritual. Consider the following examples:

- What would happen if you had an automobile and didn't use it? It would rust, the battery would go dead, axles would stiffen and not work efficiently, and when you started it (if you could start it), you would have a difficult time keeping it running.
- What happens to a house that isn't lived in? It deteriorates and eventually falls down.
- What if you had money and didn't use it? Its value would decrease, and it wouldn't purchase as much as it would have if you would have used it earlier.
- What if God had given you a gift that you didn't use? You would lose it.
- What if we had faith and didn't use it? It would weaken until it died.

Knowledge comes from external means and is transmitted to the brain. We obtain knowledge from hearing, reading, and seeing. It's taken in through our senses and transmitted to the brain. The brain is our storage bank.

Wisdom originates inward. It sorts knowledge and exerts outward. Again I could ask, what happens to knowledge that is not used? We forget it, and it becomes useless. Many highly intelligent people go through life obtaining knowledge and not putting it to profitable use. Why waste the time to obtain it if it's is not going to be used?

It is not until knowledge is exerted outward that it becomes useful. Being in sales all my life, I've been exposed to all aspects of learning and training. Some people feel that they have to know everything about their product before they feel comfortable using it. (These are those who never realize their potential for success.) Why would that be? Because you don't want to steer anyone wrong. Would it be better to have 100 percent knowledge and use 2 percent? Or have 2 percent knowledge and use 100 percent of it? The answer is the latter. Why? Because I've been studying the insurance business for more than forty years and have just scratched the surface of knowing 100 percent of all there is to know about the insurance business. If I waited to know 100 percent, I would have starved to death long ago. Time passes while you're learning. When time passes without using what you have learned, you forget. You would also miss out on the ability to handle new challenges that come along.

Is 2 percent good enough? You're never going to use more than you have, no matter the percentage. Something else happens when you use your knowledge: you remember it so much better. When you come to the point at which you are exhausting the usefulness of what you know, you continue learning. You learn as you use.

How many of us approach our Christian walk and usefulness with the attitude, *I don't know enough about it to do anybody any good. I don't want to attempt to witness or teach someone else until I know more about it.* Remember the above illustration. The same principle applies. God will not hold us accountable for what we do not know or have. He does, however, hold us accountable for what we do have.

Where do you begin your spiritual journey in fulfilling your part of the Great Commission? From where you are right now, with what knowledge you currently have. The more you use, the more you'll be given.

Christians need to apply the principle of "use and learn," not "learn then use." This may be the opposite of what you've been taught, but remember that God always applies spiritual principles that are just the opposite of worldly ways. Just think about it: Who learns the most from a Sunday school lesson or a Bible study? The teacher—the one person who does the most studying.

Godly wisdom is knowing and using the secret to happiness and prosperity for the benefit of others as well as ourselves. Many have yearned for wisdom, prosperity, and happiness all their lives. When it is not realized, they are fooled into believing that their current lifestyle, job, family, love relationship, or area where they are living is the reason they are not achieving their goals. As a result they seek to change one or all of the above. This leads to an even more unstable lifestyle and causes them to make irreversible mistakes. They may change employers, leave their families, move to another state in search of the wisdom necessary to achieve their goals. They search for years, trying different jobs, locations, or relationships. Someone somewhere has to have the answer to their dilemma. Many take this search take to the grave with them, leaving behind a life of misery, discord, and dissatisfaction, and people they've hurt along the way.

What they don't realize is that the secret to wisdom, prosperity, and happiness is not found in those places. God has hidden it within man himself the only place many fail to look. Many people spend their lives searching the world for something they have had all along when all they needed was direction in finding how to use it by tapping into the power that comes with it. We tap into it through our relationship and oneness with our Maker. God says, "Draw nigh unto me and I will draw nigh unto you" (James 4:8).

Some people find happiness in making the most of what they haven't got.

In my travels I find that the people who are the most appreciative are the ones who have the least. If you give a steak to someone who eats steak for every meal, they're not going to appreciate steak very much. However, if you give someone who is starving a loaf of bread, they will appreciate it forever.

God's Laws

God has set into motion certain laws. To attempt to change these laws is like mopping up the ocean with a sponge. It can't be done. Take, for example, the law of gravity. If I were to hold up a pencil and release it, gravity would cause it to fall down and stop on something solid. That law cannot be changed. It can temporarily be altered in simulators, but it cannot be changed.

There is the law of faith that God has placed in our lives through His Word that cannot be changed, just like the law of gravity. When we exercise our faith, it rests on something solid—the Word of God. Whether we believe it or not doesn't prevent God's promised Word from coming to pass. It changes only how we benefit by it. The degree of faith we use is up to us. We decide where the solid part it lands on is. Each time we let our faith grow, we can walk further in it.

The law of giving and receiving, or sowing and reaping, states that to reap, we must sow. We *reap* the type of seed we sow. If we plant an apple seed, we get apples. If we plant peach seeds, we get peaches. In order for that seed to multiply, it must first fall to the ground and die. God planted the seed of His only begotten Son, Jesus. God first had to give Him up and let Him die before the harvest could come—a harvest so great that we are still enjoying the fruit today, the fruit of salvation.

If a farmer buys seed, takes it home, cooks it, and then eats it, what kind of crop will he have? None. What kind of crop would we have if we eat all of our seed? We look at our finances to justify not sowing and reject the absolute function of this law. The condition of our finances does not and cannot change the law of sowing and reaping. No matter how dire we feel our need is, God will not change this law to fit your need or mine. Can you pray for God to come in supernaturally and bail you out of your current situation if you withhold? Yes. Will He? No. Why? Because it is a prayer conceived in doubt.

God gives each of us an equal amount of seeds to grow our own garden of prosperity. Many Christians don't have a harvest because they eat all the seeds for themselves instead of planting them in God's garden. You might argue that there are those who were born with silver spoons in their mouths and who have so much more. These people are smarter, more talented, and stronger, you say.

Whether or not others have more than you doesn't nullify your accountability for the seed God has given you. It is easier to hide behind the excuse that others have more and that's the reason they are so blessed. Yet nothing is further from the truth. God does not bless you because of what you have or can do. He blesses according to your own faith and what you do with what he has already given.

We cannot eat our own seeds and expect God to bless the crop.

There are many types of seeds we can sow: If we sow seeds of forgiveness, we will reap forgiveness. If we sow seeds of compassion, we will reap compassion. If we sow seeds of love, we will reap love.

If we give a dollar, surrendering it completely to God, it becomes a seed that dies to us. He waters it, and it produces fruit. It is that seed that God multiplies and sends back. The amount that He sends back is in direct proportion to what we sow. Feed your faith, and doubt will starve.

If you can't change the direction of the wind, adjust your sails.

On our life journeys, many of us are tossed about, going whichever way the wind blows. This brings us either back to where we started or to a place where we are lost and lack direction. We need to learn to use the wind in such a way to move us in the direction of the vision God has given us. We are all going through the same sea of life. Our final destination depends upon how we adjust our sails. Adjust your sails with God's Word. He doesn't guarantee that you will not encounter the wind, but He does promise that if you follow His direction, He will see you through safely to the end.

<u>Wealthy Men of the Bible</u>

"And you shall remember the LORD your God: for it is He who gives you the power to get wealth, that He may establish His covenant which He swore to your fathers, as it is this day" (Deut. 8:18).

Do you notice the Scripture above says it is God who gives us power to get wealth and not that God will give us wealth? We have a part in this process. We don't just pray and wait for God to hand it to us. We pray and believe that God will fulfill His promise if we follow His direction. Then we must move toward our goal, knowing that God will provide.

"With your [God's] wisdom and your understanding you have gained riches for yourself, and gathered gold and silver into your treasures" (Ezek. 28:4).

If we asked God for wisdom, He will give it to us. When we

obtain, we never want to forget that it is God's wisdom and not our own that has provided us with what we have obtained.

> *"And Abram was very rich in livestock, in silver, and in gold" (Gen. 13:2).*

This is most amazing. Think about where Abraham was when God made him rich. *He was in the desert.* There was no Walmart, Lowes, or industry of any kind. No telephone, mail system, stock market, or banks. *He was in the desert.*

If God could make Abraham rich out in the middle of the desert, just think of what he can do with you in your hometown. If you just look around, you will find that you have so many more resources than Abraham had. This proves that God does not need the government, state, employer, or investment firms to prosper you. It was not any of these that made Abraham rich but rather his faith in God and acting on His Word.

If we are not achieving, we make excuses and blame the area in which we live: "There is not much industry, and wages are low. I could never get ahead in this area. Besides, there is a recession, and money is in short supply." I hate to be so blunt, but that is an insult to God. God is never in short supply, and God doesn't need those sources to bless His children. When you begin to think that way, just remember Abraham. If God wants you in another location or vocation, let him do the leading. He will place you where you need to be. He wants us to exercise our faith by stepping in the water, but we must trust Him enough to take the first step.

> *"This man (Job) was the greatest of all the people of the east" (Job 1:3b).*

Job had all his possessions taken from him. The only thing he had left was what mattered the most. That was his God, who was the only one able to restore all his wealth and much more. Can God do the same for you?

"When the evening had come, there came a rich man of Arimathaea, named Joseph, who also himself had become a disciple of Jesus: This man went to Pilate, and asked for the body of Jesus" (Matt. 27:57–58).

I have heard many ministers state that God provided wealth to those in the Old Testament and not the New. What about Joseph of Arimathaea? This is New Testament. The God of the Old Testament is the same God of the New. Why say this when God's Word says differently? Because those who say this have not achieved such prosperity and therefore offer excuses instead of just accepting God's Word. Does this mean they are not men of God? No. What it does mean is that they limit and deprive themselves of blessings that God wishes them to have. They also place their own self-imposed limits on those who hear His Word and accept them as gospel.

Life is like a well; the deeper you go, the more living water you will find.

"Both riches and honor come of you, and you reign over all; In your hand is power and might; In Your hand it is to make great, and to give strength unto all" (1 Chron. 29:12).

In this prayer at the dedication of the temple, King David acknowledged the following:

- God as the source of riches and honor.
- Control is in God's hands.
- God is big enough to handle all.
- God distributes to all.

"But who am I, and who are my people, that we should be able to offer so willingly as this? For all things come of

You, and of Your own have we given You" (1 Chron. 29:14).

Here, David acknowledged that

- God is our *father* and we are his *children* and
- there is *nothing* that is not of God; all comes from Him.

Past experiences should be guideposts, not hitching posts.

Have you heard of someone stating that the reason they are not further ahead is because they have tried it before and failed or it didn't work? What they are doing is letting their bad past experiences control and limit their futures. They are using those past failures as hitching posts. That is where they hang all their excuses. Is it their past experiences that are preventing them from prospering or their own willingness to let those experiences control their lives? People, prosperous or not, all go through times of failure or times when they are holding back. What holds them back is not the problem but rather their own willingness to accept failure as the end, and then they quit trying. Failure can exist only when we stop trying.

A Practical Look at What We've Learned So Far

The terms *success* and *prosperity* are interchangeable; however, when we think in terms of success, we think of worldly success, which is *self*-centered. We sacrifice the world for self. When we think of prosperity, we think of God's promises, which are self-sacrifice and God-serving. We use self to serve the world.

We as Christians can make God's laws ineffective in our lives if we hang on to worldly thinking, depending on self. When we do this, we depend less upon God. The less we depend upon

God, the smaller our blessings. The more we depend upon God, the larger our blessings. It is when we have the least that we need to depend upon God the most.

When we store up riches for ourselves, the more we store, the more we depend upon that which we have stored and less upon God. The less we depend upon God, the more we hoard for ourselves. Doesn't this seem to come natural to us? As long as we have money in the bank stored for emergencies, we have a tendency to keep God in the background until we run short. Then we call upon Him. There is nothing wrong with saving for future events or emergencies. It is prudent to do so. However, when we depend more upon our wealth than we do upon God, we run into trouble. Loving money more than God makes money our god. Remember Joseph, who stored wheat when Egypt was doing well for seven years so it could be used when a seven-year famine came? Had he not stored, many would have starved. So God expects us to be good stewards and put aside, but we are not to put aside for ourselves what belongs to God. That is placing our riches before God.

Hoarding is always caused by fear and doubt. Fear and doubt are the opposite of faith. God can honor only faith. He cannot honor fear or doubt. Fear causes us to withhold from God. When we fear, we empower those things in our lives that hold us back from believing in and serving God. They are self-destructive.

- Fear causes loss.
- Faith causes gain.
- Fear brings the problem.
- Faith brings the solution.
- Fear always looks back.
- Faith always looks forward.
- Fear always brings defeat.
- Faith always brings victory.
- Fear hates God.

- Faith loves God.
- Fear brings worry.
- Faith brings courage.
- Fear sees a tunnel at the end of every light.
- Faith sees the light at the end of every tunnel.
- Fear sees doubt.
- Faith sees assurance.
- Fear sees an eternal lake of fire at the end of life.
- Faith sees a mansion in heaven.
- Fear sees the sickness and the disease
- Faith sees the healing.
- Fear says *I can't*.
- Faith says *I can*.
- Fear says *I won't*.
- Faith says *I will*.
- Fear sees darkness.
- Faith sees light.
- Fear sees despair.
- Faith sees prosperity.
- Fear weakens.
- Faith strengthens.
- Fear attacks the Word of God.
- Faith uses the Word of God.

What do you see? What do you want to see? Doesn't it make good sense to let go of your fear and cling to your faith?

- Always remember the only ones who can look through your eyes are you and God.
- You will see what you want to see and look where you want to look.
- You cannot blame someone else for what you see.
- If you see fear, you are not allowing God to look through your eyes with you.

- If you see faith, you are allowing God to look through your eyes with you.
- If you've been experiencing many bad things and you're living a life of defeat, perhaps it's because you're constantly looking at fear. Turn your eyes from fear and put them on faith.
- If where you've looked in the past is not your intended destination, turn and look in the direction of faith, or your past will be your destination.

All fear is that God's promises may not come to pass.

Turning Storm Clouds into Chariots

An eagle sits on a crag and watches the sky as it is filling with blackness and the forked lightning plays up and down. He is sitting perfectly still ... Until he begins to feel the burst of the breeze and knows the hurricane has struck him. Then he swings his breast to the storm, and uses the storm to go up to the sky. Away he goes, borne upward upon it. That is what God wants of every one of His children to be more than conqueror and turn the storm cloud into a chariot. (*Sunday School Times*)

When storm clouds come our way, we have a tendency to run and hide or go the other direction for fear of the storm. Remember in chapter 2 when God sent His angels to build a wall of protection around those that are His. He will only let through that hedge that which will not destroy us but that which will make us stronger. Knowing that we are not facing storms in life on our own power but on God's power gives us the courage to face the storm and move in its direction. Doing so with God's help causes us to use the storm to rise above it to heights unattainable had we not had the storm.

Looking back on my own life, I can see that my spiritual

growth was the strongest not in the times of calm but the times of storm. The storm gives us strength in areas we didn't even know we needed. But God knows our needs better than we do. Having faith in Him through the storms, we know that He will bring us out to the other side.

Remember when Jesus got into the boat with the disciples and told them they were going to the other side of the Sea of Galilee. Jesus was asleep in the back when a storm arose so fierce that the disciples thought they were going to die. Waking Jesus up, they accused Him of not caring whether or not they perished. Jesus reprimanded them for their lack of faith. Why? Because Jesus had already told them they were going to the other side. They doubted Him, just as we do when storms or problems come into our lives. We feel they are going to harm or destroy us.

Let's just look at our lives as being in a boat on a rough sea. The sea is sometimes calm and many times rough because of storms. The storms are sometimes so powerful that we realize we cannot get to the other side on our own power. We are being blown about from side to side and whichever way the wind blows, causing us to get lost. Many people are lost but don't know it. They think they know the way and insist on going in the direction they think is right. *"There is a way which seems right unto a man, but its end is the way of death" (Prov. 14:12).*

On the other hand, there are those who come to the conclusion that they cannot navigate the waters of life alone and that they can never reach the other side without guidance of someone who knows the way, someone who can quell the storms with a spoken word. They see Jesus standing on the shore with outstretched hands, wanting to show the way. They stop and pick him up (praying the prayer of salvation), and He gets into the boat with them and says, "We will go to the other side." (Christ comes into our hearts and makes a home with us, and our final destination is now heaven.) With Him aboard, no matter how high the waters get, they will never overflow into the boat. No matter how great the storm, we have the One and only One who can say to the storm, "Peace be still," and the storms obey. He may not stop a particular storm in your life that you are going through, but rest assured He promises to see us through it. Remember, Jesus was in the boat with the disciples through the storm. Jesus is the only one who knows the way to the other side. Folks, that is love that is assurance. With such assurance, you can do all things through Jesus Christ, who strengthens you (Phil. 4:13). He is the captain of our souls and the sailor's compass.

It will always cost you more to say *no* to God than it will to say *yes*.

Chapter 4 Action Project

I will do the following:

1. Thank God for the things He has already given me and not complain about what I don't have.
2. Recognize that I have physical limits. God, however, has no limits, physical or spiritual. If God is in me, then I too have no limits, and all things are possible.
3. Practice sowing seeds, realizing that it is impossible to grow a crop if I eat all my own seeds.
4. Recognize that the seed I sow is the seed that will grow.

Chapter 5: Needs and Greeds

WE have all encountered problems in our lives, even Christians. Being a Christian doesn't exempt one from having problems. If we were to look through the eyes of God and see why many of our problems exist, we would find that it is because we have created most of them ourselves. There are problems we didn't create, yet we have to deal with them. A problem not dealt with wins the battle. One of the main problems we create in our businesses, churches, and homes is never determining the difference between *need* and *greed*. Remember the internal and the external. We use the external world to satisfy self and our internal powers to meet the needs of the world.

When we read God's Word, we are looking through the eyes of God and seeing our faults and needs and blessings. When we let God look through our eyes, we can then see the needs of others and how we can be a blessing to them.

God never reacts to our need. He reacts to our faith.

Greed originates internally and uses others to minister to self. Needs originate externally. When we conduct ourselves in ways to meet our greeds, we are reducing or eliminating the potential to meet the needs of others, such as our employers, churches, families, and friends. I would like to propose a challenge to all readers: the next time you make a purchase, ask yourself, "Do I need it, or do I greed it?"

Does this mean we should not want anything to satisfy ourselves? No, not at all. What we have for ourselves is what God gives us as a reward for meeting the needs of others, and it is the fruit of our labors, not our reason for living.

We build either better Sunday schools or better prison cells.

It is much easier to minister and guide someone in a Sunday school than in a prison. Sunday schools prepare us for making good, sound decisions that will move us forward in life. Prison cells punish for making wrong decisions. Those with Antichrist who are moving hard to remove God from our educational system are actually creating job security for those who build prisons. When we remove God from any sector of society, the only outcome can be chaos. Sunday schools or prisons—which is better?

The Difference Between Worldly and Prosperous (A Review)

- A worldly person is driven by self-fulfillment and self-satisfaction and thinks he owns everything he has.
- A prosperous person realizes everything comes from God.
- A worldly person sees his own needs.
- A prosperous person sees the needs of others.
- A worldly person has learned how to make money.
- A prosperous person has learned how to give it.
- A worldly person achieves great things.

- A prosperous person serves others and helps them to achieve their goals.
- A worldly person says *the world owes me* and serves self (ministering to self).
- A prosperous person says *I owe God* and serves Him (ministering to the world).
- A worldly person says *I did it.*
- A prosperous person says *God did it.*
- A worldly person loves things that serve self.
- A prosperous person loves God and serves others.

"And he said naked came I from my mother's womb, and naked shall I return. The Lord gives and the Lord has taken away; blessed be the name of the Lord" (Job 1:21).

Money Needed

Being in the business that I am (church property and liability insurance) has enabled me to see churches of many shapes, sizes, and forms and has allowed me to get an idea of the financial strength of the church. What I have noticed in all churches is that there are times when needs arise for additional funding for things such as youth projects, equipment, furniture, building additions, or even just paying the bills.

When such needs arise, I often hear, "Does anyone have any ideas how we will raise the money?" They inevitably look to outside sources and suggest perhaps a hoagie sale, ask for donations for the project, or have a dinner to invite the public and charge a nominal fee. "After all," they reason, "they have to eat somewhere, and we may as well make some money at the same time while giving them a good deal."

Even though God gives us a mission to go out and minister

to the world, doing the above is going into the world to get the unsaved to minister to the needs of the saved. If they can get those outside the church to meet the financial needs of the church, they would not have to dig into their own pockets.

The need for these would go away
if the people of God would tithe and pray.

Churches that are having the most financial troubles are those that look to the unsaved to pay for the church's needs. That's like going to our neighbors, knocking on their doors, and asking them to contribute to help pay our phone or electric bills. Yes, there are churches in which funds have not been managed properly or the leadership got ahead of God and made decisions that strapped the church financially. However, the majority of financial troubles are experienced because the congregation does not tithe and pray. When I hear that a church needs repairs, "but we cannot afford it, even if it is a hazard to the safety of worshipers," it's a strong indication that they care more for their money than their worshipers' well-being. It is not that they don't have it. It is that they want to keep it and use it for their own needs rather than give it to the Lord's work. It may be that the church really is too small, but we have to wonder, are they not able to meet ministry needs because they are too small, or are they too small because they will not meet the ministry needs?

Shortly after I became a Christian, I prayed for God's direction in my life. "God, what do you want me to do?" I placed myself in the hand of God and said, "God, use me." That week I was asked to serve on the board of trustees for the church we were attending. This board exists for the purpose of taking care of the business of the church, which includes handling all financial matters. It had quickly come to my attention that the church was having trouble paying the pastor's salary and the monthly bills. I asked how much it would take to pay off the mortgage and what the payments were. The answer shocked me. I was told that the church was paid off and owed nothing. I may have been a young Christian, but I knew what the problem was. It wasn't a lack of people or money; the problem was that the congregation wasn't tithing. Less than a handful were bearing the brunt of the expenses for the whole. The rest were willing to let them.

Some people think they are worth a lot of money because they have it.

Don't you find sometimes that people who have a lot of money let it change their personal value? This is a tricky misconception that fools a lot of people. Think about it: when they die, the money stays behind. With that type of thinking, the one that has the most possessions or money becomes more valuable. They may be able to purchase more, but their personal value does not change. This concept is popular worldly thinking. The world looks at the outside: what can that person do for me, or how can that person help me? If they can't, they are of no value.

Remember the difference between *worldly* and *godly*? A person's worth or value does not come by external means, and neither is it calculated by how much they have. It comes internally and is generated from within and exerted outward to meet the needs of others.

Do you want people to determine your value or worth by how much money you have or don't have? Or do you want relationships with people based upon how they value you as a person? This is what we all really want. We want to be loved or needed for our internal personal value and not by what we have (external). Then when we die, the personal value stays and lives within the hearts of others we have helped along the way.

125

God Owns All

> *"And God blessed them, and God said unto them, be fruitful, and multiply, and replenish the earth, and subdue it: and have dominion over the fish of the sea and over the fowl of the air, and over every living thing that moves upon the earth" (Gen. 1:28).*

With the blessing of God, we bear fruit, have children, and control the earth. To *have dominion* means to rule the earth and all living things. Notice this command was given to God's children. We are responsible for God's property. For some reason we seem to want to pass that responsibility to the unsaved and surrender our inheritance. Those who declare ownership control those who occupy.

> *"And God said, See, I have given you every herb bearing seed, which is on the face of all the earth, and every tree whose fruit yields seed; to you it shall be for food" (Gen. 1:29).*

God gave us the harvest. God also gave us the seed from the harvest to replant. We receive the fruit of the replanting.

Remember, fruit comes after the seed is planted. Within the fruit are more seeds to replant, and the rest is ours to enjoy as the fruit of our labors. We cannot refuse to plant the seed and pray that God will give us the fruit. That is making a mockery of God. You see, God has already instructed us in the way He will bless us with the fruit: plant the seed. We, like little children, refuse to listen to God, and then we ask God to bless our disobedience. We have a tendency to look at planting seed as a loss. We need to realize that the fruit we desire is already contained in the seed. In order to see the fruit harvest, we must plant the seed. Unless the seed falls to the ground and dies, it cannot bear fruit. When we plant it, it dies to us. Only then will the fruit come.

"And to every beast of the earth, and to every bird of the air, and to everything that creeps on the earth, in which there is life, I have given every green herb for food; and it was so" (Gen. 1:30).

Every living thing is given to man. All is given for food for man. All come from God.

"And the gold of the land is good: bdellium and the onyx stone are there" (Gen. 2:12).

Gold money is good. If money is evil, it is because we make it that way, not God. What we use it for or misuse it for is what makes it evil. Only when it is used according to God's instructions is it good. If you don't have enough money, it's not because God does not want you to have it. He made it for His children. Could the reason we don't have enough to meet our needs be because we refuse to follow God's direction in obtaining it? For example, we've all seen movies about pirates who plundered villages to steal their valuables, including gold. They found an island upon which to bury their treasure. Why did they do that? Well, they didn't have banks to keep it in while they went out to get more. The burial place was their secret bank. They would, however, draw a map with directions on how to find it. They kept the map in a secret place. We've all dreamed of finding such a map—a map that would direct us to a treasure that would set us up for life.

Let's say you found such a map. It pinpoints exactly where the treasure is. However, it is at an inconvenient place and would cost you to get there. It would require you to get out of your comfort zone. You would have to do without some conveniences to get it. Because of the inconvenience to you, would you lay the map aside and say, "I'll dig for it in a more convenient area"? You could dig up the whole world and never find it. It's in only one place the place you refuse to look. You'd have to be brain-dead if you did this. You'd never lay the map aside. You would treasure it and follow its direction to the tee.

God has buried treasure and made you a map to find exactly where it is. After all, it is His treasure; He owns all gold and silver. He buried it just for you. He is the only one in the world who knows where it is, and He tells you exactly how to get it. But you lay the map aside and dig in convenient areas all over the world in an attempt to find it and convince yourself that God does not want you to have it.

The map is the Bible. The treasure is buried within the heart of every Christian. We refuse to believe it is buried there. If you really want the treasure God has for you, stop digging where you like to dig, start reading the map, follow it, and then dig where He directs with precise accuracy. Our faith in the One that made the map is what releases the treasure. Looking for God's treasure outside your own heart is like wanting to lose weight by watching someone else exercise.

> *"But of the tree of knowledge of good and evil, you shall not eat: for in the day you shall eat of you shall surely die" (Gen. 2:17).*

Then God made Eve, and she convinced Adam to eat of the tree from which God told him not to eat. We make decisions every day to listen to God or someone else. If we choose not to listen to God, we remove ourselves from receiving the blessings of God.

We are where we are in life because of our own choosing. You may feel this is a brazen statement, and it may shut you off. Let's analyze it. Motivational speaker and best-selling author Norman Vincent Peale once said, "We are a sum total of all our thoughts." I have given this statement a lot of thought. God says that without vision, people perish. In other words, what we envision consumes our thoughts. Now, do our thoughts control the vision, or does our vision control our thoughts?

If our thoughts control our vision, the vision comes from our own minds. It is the vision that comes from God that needs to control our thoughts. What dominates our minds is what comes to pass in our lives. We need to recognize God's vision and let that vision dominate our thoughts. Then and only then will God's will come to pass in our lives. Whether or not we reach that goal or even move toward it depends upon if we put our minds to it. In other words, we can have a vision and ignore it. We ignore it because we have other things in our lives we consider more important. The things we consider the most important in our lives are what we decide to focus our thoughts on. Whether we succeed or fail in achieving God's will in our lives and prosper is not a mandate but a decision we make.

It's hard to concentrate on something through to its completion because of circumstances in our lives that deter our thinking and move us off track. It may be that someone else's actions derailed us and put us where we are currently, but we don't have to stay there. Whether or not we stay is of our own choosing. If you are in an undesirable position right now because someone has done you wrong, you don't have to stay there. Getting out of that position is your responsibility. Are you going to stay there, or are you going to move forward in faith toward your vision?

> *"Then to Adam he said because you have heeded the voice of your wife, and have eaten from the tree, of which I commanded you, saying You shall not eat of it: cursed is the ground for your sake; in toil you shall eat of it all the days of your life; Both thorns and thistles it brings forth for you … In the sweat of thy face shall eat bread, till you return to the ground" (Gen. 3:17–19).*

If we want to eat, we must work.

Money Problems

To worldly people, the closest thing to their hearts is their money. If money is where your heart is, your heart has no more value than the amount of money you have. To a Christian, money is the hardest thing to give up. Remember, we are making a transformation from the world. To the worldly person, everything in life revolves around money. The work of Jesus is given up for money or for the right to keep or use it as one desires. To a Christian, everything in life revolves around Jesus. We are willing to give up money for the work of Jesus. The closest thing to our hearts is tested and proven by what we give, not by what we have. But we condition ourselves to depend more upon money than upon God. You can entrust God with your soul, but can He trust you with His money?

If we consider money ours and not God's, we are more reluctant to give it up. Why is it that we can place our lives in the hands of our Savior and know that He has removed us from the penalty of sin by His forgiveness? We trust Him with our eternal souls so that when we die we will go to live with Him forever. Now, when it comes to our money, we don't believe Him when He says that we cannot outgive Him. How can we have enough faith to believe He will save our souls, which we cannot see, and we don't trust Him with our money, which we can see?

We can depend upon God, but can God depend upon you? If you ask God for something in prayer and expect an answer, can God ask something of you and expect an answer? What was your most recent response when asked to do something for God or His work? Was it one of the following:

- "I would love to, but I just don't have time." You are not saying no to a person but to God.
- "Why don't you ask so and so? They are more talented/have more time/are a stronger Christian."

• "I don't know anything about that area of ministry."

Whatever the excuse, just think about this: Remember the next time you get on your knees and pray for God to answer a prayer. You remind God that He said, *anything we asked He will give it*, and we expect God to get busy and answer that prayer ASAP. If God gave you the same excuse for not answering your prayer as you give Him for not answering His request, how many prayers would you have answered?

When it comes to making a decision in our lives or our ministries, before we spend, do we ask if we have enough money? Or do we ask if it is God's will? Which do we find ourselves depending upon to provide—our treasury or God's promise?

When you've been elected by your church to handle the money that is given, you need to be a good steward in dispersing it for God's work. Being a good steward requires you to be a good student of His Word. In turn, being a good student of His Word requires you to believe in His Word. Believing in His Word requires you to believe not the physical, what you can see, but what we can believe through Christ's promises.

Most churches that are going nowhere in ministry and are struggling to keep their doors open find that a member or members on their decision-making body do not believe or practice this. So when a problem is brought to their attention, such as the need for a new carpet or a new roof, they take one of two actions:

1. If there isn't enough money in the treasury, they decide not to do it because they say they can't afford it. Their faith is in their treasury and not in God. Faith is limited to only what they can see.

2. They go to their knees and ask God, "Is it Your will?" and abide by the answer to that prayer. They

> know that if God wants it, He will make a means to
> pay for it even if they cannot see it in their treasury.

If we can find the faith, God can find a way. God rewards according to our faith and does not limit our faith; we do. Thus, He will not go any further than our faith will reach. I am not suggesting you test your faith by going out to the end of a cliff and take another step, expecting God to protect you. You may get to heaven quicker, but you will still die from the fall. The Lord warns us about tempting God. *"Do not tempt the Lord thy God: (Matt: 4:7).*

God will always take us as far as our faith will go. God will never take us further than our faith will reach. If we place a limit on faith, we place a limit on God.

Important: We are talking about active faith and not passive faith.

Passive Faith—Faith in which we pray, believing and waiting for God to answer our prayer without our action.

Passive faith is a safety net we provide for ourselves so that if God does not answer our prayers, we won't embarrass ourselves by claiming He did and people won't think less of us. Is this because of faith or doubt?

Active Faith—When we pray in faith, believing, we not only pray knowing that God will answer our prayers, but we also take action on that prayer.

Again, *without works, faith is dead*. We must exercise our faith as an active faith, acting upon it while knowing that God is in it. Knowing this, why do we then present the need to others, expecting the needs will be met through them? If we found the faith, then God expects us to act upon our own faith. What I mean by that is it is *our own pockets* that God expects us to reach into first. It is then that God honors our faith and becomes active in the situation by placing the need in the hearts of others so that they can act on their own faith, thus fulfilling the vision by using His resources, which may or may not go outside the walls of the church. Faith grows faith. Faith grows ministries. God always keeps His Word. When acted upon in this manner, it doesn't make any difference if there is not currently enough in the treasury of the local congregation to cover the need. There is always enough in God's Kingdom to cover any and all of our needs according to His riches in glory, not our riches. God's treasury never runs dry. Never. He will never stop giving until we stop believing. *But the question is, do you believe?* This is what separates the dreamers from the achievers.

When we walk through life, we are walking in our physical strength and walking by sight. When you reach the point where you cannot go any farther in the physical realm, *just take one more step.* That is where Christ will meet you. That is the step we are taking in faith.

It's like coming to the edge of our own capabilities, and we cannot go any further without the Lord. Faith is when you can look at that next step and see the hand of Christ. When you take that step, you are stepping into His hand, which nobody else can see but you. When you do so, you are leaving the safety of the physical realm, which you depend upon so much, and stepping into His promise. Now you are depending completely upon Him for your security. You are now in the hand of Jesus. He'll take you where He wants you to go or carry you to the vision which He placed on your heart.

Do we make decisions based upon the following questions?

- How many people do we have in the church, or how much income they are making?
- Are people laid off?
- Is our area economically depressed?
- Do people have low-paying jobs?
- Do we believe only that which we can see, or do we believe in God for that which we can't see?

Ask yourself the same question for your own household. I have heard well-meaning ministers say the reason certain things aren't being done that need to be done is because people have limited incomes or low-paying jobs or because they are laid off and cannot afford to give any more. That is undoubtedly true. However, what they are actually saying is that God is dependent upon our employers, the government, state, or economy and cannot supply beyond those sources. You see, they are confining God to their church people instead of growing the faith of the people to reach beyond the walls of the church to the true source—God. It is not that God can't; it is because we don't have the faith to believe that God can. When we confine our thinking to the people that bring in the funds, we are confining our ministry to the walls of the church. God's church does not have walls; our buildings do. Don't make the mistake of building walls around God.

If we believe only what we can see, we have already limited our blessings to that which we can see. Don't get discouraged because you cannot see it. Most of the blessings God has for us are found in what we cannot see. We are slaves to the limits we set in our own minds. God sets no limits. God cannot bless us further than our faith will go.

People who never do more than they get paid to do never get paid for more than they do. People who do more than what they are paid to do will eventually get paid for more than what they do. Place yourself in the position of an employer. Your employees are trying to make ends meet and get raises or promotions. They want to get ahead so they can have comfortable lives. You ask one of your employees to do something, and his or her response is, "I don't get paid to do that, so I can't be expected to do it." They come to work just before starting time and leave right at quitting time. They do their job but no more. This person works because he or she has to and not because he or she wants to. Now, as an employer you would only tolerate this person and may even look for ways to replace him or her. Thus the employee restricts his or her own chances of a raise or a promotion.

You have another employee who sees that something needs done and even though nobody is looking, he or she just go ahead and do it. He or she comes in early enough to be at his or her work station before starting time, and if there is something undone at quitting time, that person stay a few minutes to make sure it is done and done right. This person does it even if he or she doesn't get paid to do it. This person works because he or she wants to and not because he or she has to. As an employer, you see the value of this person and look for ways to make sure you keep him or her.

As you contemplate salary increases or promotions, which of the two employees would you offer the raise in pay or promotion? Number two, of course. This employee shows initiative and is concerned about your business not because of what he or she can get out of it, but because he or she wants to see the business succeed and move forward. This person knows that in order for your business to move forward, you need to be presented to the public in a positive manner, and he or she wants to do his or her part. Yes, that is the person I want to promote. That person has proven him- or herself to be worthy. It is that person who will eventually get paid for more than what he or she does.

Yet when trying to obtain a job, too many people do everything they can to prove they're worthy and the best choice for the job. Once they get the job, however, they try to get out of work and look for ways to rest, cut corners, or leave quickly. Don't be like employee number one. Become like number two. Do more than you are expected in everything you do. If you are expected to give a certain amount, give more.

Apply this concept to God's work when you're asked to do something in the church or for someone else. Do it with pleasure because you want to and not out of resentment or because you have to. God wants willing servants. God rewards His servants according to what they do and not what they refuse to do. Most Christians go through their Christian walks just doing what they have to do and get by, even though it is self-defeating. They are serving out of necessity and not because they want to or want to see the Kingdom get ahead. They just want to get their feet in the door to heaven and nothing else. Now, look at your Christian walk through the eyes of the employer and God. Which type of person do you see yourself as? The decision of which person you are is not one of chance but of choice.

Questions and Answers

Q: Is God sitting on the throne, waiting for us to step out of line so He can punish us?

A: No. God is sitting on the throne waiting to bless us. He is asking us to give Him the opportunity. We must place ourselves in a position to be blessed by exercising our faith. ("Without works, faith is dead," James 2:17). God's pleasure is fulfilled in your hands being full.

Q: Does He wish for His property to be used for evil?

A: No. He created it to be used for good.

Q: Does He want us dependent upon the world to supply our needs?

A: No. He calls upon us to supply the world's needs.

Q: Does God despise the wealthy?

A: No. God gave man the power to create wealth.

Q: If God truly wants us to prosper, why are there so many hurting Christians?

A: Many Christians hurt not because they did something wrong but because they give themselves to suffer with and for Christ for the benefit of others. Many other Christians hurt because they do not believe God can or will keep His Word and therefore withhold from God. When we withhold from God, God withholds from us.

A pessimist sees the difficulty in every opportunity. An optimist sees the opportunity in every difficulty.

You cannot live a perfect day without doing something for someone who will never be able to repay you.

Everyone Is Battling Something

No matter, what your battle is today, God is with you, will not forsake you, and will walk you out of your valley to the mountaintop of victory! Too often we focus on the battle and not the victory. Too often we look only at the circumstances and not the One who promised us victory over our circumstances.

Several disciples of Jesus were in a boat one day when a great storm came upon them. The winds began to blow, the rain began to fall, and the sky darkened. All they could see was the storm. They became consumed with their circumstances and woke Jesus, who was sleeping in the boat, and asked Him to help them. Seeing their fear, Jesus, in an act of compassion, made the storm go away. The same Jesus who made the storm go away for His disciples is the same Jesus who can make the storm in your life go away. And if He doesn't take it away, He'll see you through to the other side. We have the Lord living within us in the person of the Holy Spirit. When we don't feel Him moving in our life, He's at rest, waiting to be called upon.

Chapter 5 Action Project

I will do the following:

1. I will ask myself with every purchase I make, "Is this a need, or is this a greed?"
2. If my answer is greed, I will not make the purchase.
3. I will use the money I would have spent on the purchase to plant a seed to help someone in need.
4. I will pray for God to help me concentrate on meeting the needs of others and trust God to meet my needs.

Chapter 6: Rules of Engagement

HAVE you made the decision yet to follow God's direction? If you haven't, don't read any farther. It won't do any good. Go back and read the last chapter again. If you have decided to follow His direction, read on.

**Life itself can't give you joy
unless you really will it.
Life just gives you time and space;
it's up to you to fill it.**

Do you find yourself going through life waiting to become happy or for joy to find you? Do you think you got cheated in life and consider yourself of little value? Do you feel that you got the short end of the stick? If you answered yes, you may be looking at life as though it owes you, like it's not producing your expected outcome. Stop thinking this way before you waste your life, unable to enjoy its valuable blessings.

Life is a gift from God. God gives us time and space to enjoy it. His intention is for you to prosper and enjoy life. But you must want it enough to go after it. I would encourage you not to look for joy and peace to come from life or other people. Joy and peace are generated from within. It's up to you to push the start button on the generator. You're not here by chance or by choice but of God.

Caution: don't look for loopholes in God's Word to justify your unbelief.

God has given us minds with which to make decisions. He didn't give them to us to be our masters but our servants. The mind that does not have a vision of the future only replays the painful memories of the past. Replaying our past painful memories serves as a roadblock, preventing God from releasing blessings into our lives. Only you can remove that roadblock. Binding our futures with our pasts causes us to look for loopholes in God's Word to justify our lack of faith and unbelief.

Before the start of the Persian Gulf War, reports Shepherd, Kohut, and Sweet, "Israel's Chief Rabbi Mordechi Eliyahu ruled that ultra-Orthodox Jewish men could break Jewish law forbidding men from shaving in case of an Iraqi chemical attack so gas masks could fit properly over their beards. Eliyahu urged bearded men to carry scissors in their pocket in case they needed to shave quickly." They continued, saying that "although Jewish law regarding the Sabbath forbids even simple physical activities, such as turning on the radio, the threat of Iraqi missile attacks ... sent Israel's chief rabbis scrambling to the Scriptures for a loophole so Orthodox Jews could listen to the news for warnings. The rabbis ruled that leaving the radio on during the Sabbath was permissible—provided it was on low volume."

"If there is a real alarm, you can turn up the volume," explained Religious Affairs Minister Avner Shaki, "but in a nonconventional manner, with a stick or with your elbow. Controlling the volume in a different manner still marks the Sabbath as different from the rest of the week."

Does God create laws that are detrimental to our own safety or existence? Christ is the fulfillment of the law and in Him we find rest. There were so many laws adding on to the original intent of God's promises found in the Mosaic Covenant of Deuteronomy 28–30. Instead of looking for loopholes in God's

Word, we should look for ways to increase our faith. Remember that God does not respond to our needs, doubts, and fears. *He responds to our faith.* For example, God does not respond to our sickness; He responds to our faith in Him to heal our sickness. He does not respond to hunger in the world; He responds to faith of God's people who feed the hungry.

Do you really want to prosper? If so, prosperity is yours if you are God's.

You can depend on Jesus, but can He depend on you? The Lord must be able to depend on you so that when He calls, you will answer. The question isn't what I want for myself but what God wants for me. Perhaps the reason we don't place ourselves in God's hands is we're afraid He'll want something for us that we don't want, ask us to do something we don't want to do, or ask us to go someplace we don't want to go. To be used by God, we must trust in Him and dedicate our all to Him. What we withhold from Him, He cannot bless. He can bless only that which we give to Him for His cause.

Rules of Engagement

In order to claim the prosperity God wants us to have, we must claim it according to His Word, where He gives us instructions to follow. Prosperity has eluded many because they don't follow God's instructions.

Rule 1: Recognize the Lord as the Supplier of All Needs

Sometimes we attempt to justify where we are in life by saying to ourselves, "God does not want me to prosper." Is this self-sacrifice or a lack of belief? We tend to think this way after we've tried and failed to get ahead and have fallen short of what we want out of life. The problem is we're trying to do it on our own. We don't have the power to reach beyond our physical limitations. When we have Jesus, we are not alone. Jesus shows us how to use God's power in our lives and ministries.

"And my God shall supply all your needs according to his riches in glory by Christ Jesus" (Phil. 4:19).

Shall, not may. *All*, not some. By Christ Jesus, not ourselves.

> *"Jesus said to him, If you can believe, all things are possible to him who believes" (Mark 9:23).*

We have a part: we must *believe*. Again *all*, not some. We can either operate on our own power and fail or operate on God's power and succeed. Many choose to operate on their own power because they can believe only in what they can see. It's the easy road and doesn't require faith, only physical knowledge and strength. To operate on God's power doesn't come naturally to us because it's supernatural, requiring faith in the unseen, what we cannot see.

Man rewards sight and not faith (natural). God rewards faith and not sight (supernatural). This comes by choice, not chance. It's a decision we all make. Which did you choose? If you have not chosen the supernatural, you need to increase your faith. Faith comes by hearing and hearing by the Word of God (Rom. 10:17). Get into the Word.

> *"Then you say in your heart, my power and the might of my hand have gained me this wealth. But thou shall remember the LORD your God: for it is He who gives you power to get wealth, that He may establish His covenant which He swore unto your fathers, as it is this day" (Deut. 8:17–18).*

As Christians, we are learning to put worldly ways aside and choose God's ways, which are just the opposite of what we have been taught in the world. We must transform our thinking from the natural to the supernatural.

*"And God is able to make all grace abound toward you;
that you, always having all sufficiency in all things, may
abound for every good work" (2 Cor.9:8a).*

All, always, every, shall, never are absolutes. When we see them in secular publications, we know a false statement follows. There is nothing in this world for which there are no exceptions.

In my thirteen years in management with a large insurance company, I hired and trained representatives for sales. Prior to their being able to sell insurance they had to pass the state examination. This required hard study. When they were ready to take the state test, I would instruct them, "When you see any of these words on the test—*all, always, every, shall* and *never*—scratch that as being the answer. The reason being that there are no absolutes in this world in rules and regulations." Only in God's Word are these absolutes found and found to be reliable.

and

Prosperity is a matter of luck. Ask any failure.

It really does my heart good to see someone prosper and get ahead. It offers comfort and assurance to those who are still trying. However, there are those who will look for a reason why others are getting ahead and they aren't. Instead of admitting there may be something they're doing wrong, they make an excuse why others are achieving more than they are. They say, "In order to get ahead, you have to lie, cheat, or steal or be just plain lucky." What they're actually doing is revealing their own inadequacies. They're admitting the only way they can see themselves getting ahead is to lie, cheat, or steal, and they haven't been lucky so far. Instead of admitting they have a weakness that needs to be overcome in order to achieve, they attempt to draw others down to their level. Doing so offers them a reason not to try. They see themselves as better for it because, after all, they wouldn't think to lie, cheat, or steal like those ahead of them.

Rule 2: Believe God Wants You to Prosper

> *"Though he heap up silver like dust, and piles up clothing like clay; He may pile it up, but the just will wear it, and the innocent will divide the silver" (Job 27:16–17).*

God has given us answers to the puzzle of life in pieces scattered throughout Scriptures. Each piece contains part of a solution to life's problems. It is up to us to find the pieces we need and put them where they fit so we can enjoy a complete, prosperous life.

> *"Most assuredly, I say unto you. He who believes on me, the works that I do he will do also; and greater works than these he will do; because I go to my Father. And whatever you shall ask in my name, that I will do, that the Father may be glorified in the Son. If you ask anything in my name, I will do it" (John 14:12–14).*

We may unknowingly ask for something that would be harmful to us or those close to us. God knows all. If the prayer we pray will harm us, God may not answer that prayer. If we ask something that goes against God's Word, He cannot answer that prayer in a positive way. We learn to pray in accordance with God's will, but we really must believe in God's Word and apply it to our lives to have enough faith to pray that way.

> *"Beloved I pray that you may prosper in all things and be in good health, just as your soul prospers" (3 John 2).*

If we aren't prospering, it isn't because God doesn't want us to. It's because we refuse to follow His instructions or accept the responsibility that goes with it.

The key to prosperity is in our souls, not our minds. Does the mind control the heart and soul, or do the heart and soul control the mind? This is not a trick question. Let's think it through. The mind is a storage bank for information we feed into it through our senses smell, hearing, taste, sight, and touch. This is our conscious mind. Our subconscious is on automatic, busy controlling the bodily functions and storing information. Somewhere in our subconscious mind is stored everything we have ever experienced through those senses. The mind controls the physical, or the natural, world in and around us.

The heart and soul, on the other hand, transcend the mind and enter the spiritual, the world of the unseen or the supernatural. This is the arena where we meet God. God says where our treasure is, that is where our heart is. When we walk by faith, we are stepping into the supernatural.

When we were without Christ in our hearts, our minds were in control, taking care of self with little or no thought to the supernatural. Our minds created the vision of us for future success or failure. We then lived out what we believed in our minds. We were also limited to what the mind could produce. We were governed by what we could see, and we believed what we saw.

When we met Jesus and became born of the Spirit, we surrendered the natural to the supernatural. Our hearts and souls were given to God. This transition must take place if we are ever to receive the blessings God has in store for us in this world and the world to come. As Christians, we seek God for a vision. Our hearts and souls now dictate to the mind what to study, store, and use, so we live out what we believe in the heart. We are living by faith. God says that without vision, people perish. Now we can see what we believe with no physical limitations. We are now working on God's promise and not our ability, without spiritual limitations. God, working within us, accomplishes the vision He cast for us. Our part is to believe, trust, and obey.

> *"By humility and the fear of the LORD are riches, and honor, and life" (Prov. 22:4).*

True humility and respect for the Lord lead a man to riches, honor, and a long life. Humility and respect are requirements, not options.

> *"And whosoever exalts himself shall be humbled; and he who humbles himself will be exalted" (Matt. 23:12).*

Humility can be misunderstood. Some claim humility because they have a talent and have to be begged to use it, or they are rich and pretend to be poor. That is not humility. Humility is not thinking too highly of yourself, realizing your talent comes from God, and using it for His purpose above your own. Humility is knowing that you are no better than anyone else just because you may have more money, possessions, or talent. We are all equal in the eyes of God.

> *"I love those who love me; and those who seek me diligently will find me. Riches and honor are with me; enduring riches and righteousness" (Prov. 8:17–18).*

When Jesus comes in, riches and honor come with Him, which means if we have Jesus we have (present tense) riches and honor. We know that God owns all worldly as well as heavenly riches. When we are born again and ask Jesus to come into our hearts, He comes in to live there. When He comes in, does He leave all His wealth with the Father? No, He brings it with Him. God can live anywhere in the universe, but He chose to live in the hearts of His children. We find ourselves praying for these things every day, all the days of our lives, as if they are out of reach. We are praying for things that Jesus has already given us. He tells us He wants to give them to us. In God's Word are

His instructions as to how He will release them to us. But it's easier to pray than to read and heed His instructions. He releases His riches according to the faith we exercise. You've heard the saying, "If all else fails, pray." Wrong advice. Seek God *first* in any situation you face, not as a last resort.

I consider myself a macho guy. Macho guys think they know more than they really do. If you're a macho guy, you'll use your strength and mind to do what you can in any given situation. One Christmas when my children were growing up, I purchased something mechanical as a gift. I took it out of the box, separated the pieces, and put it together. When I was done, I found that not only didn't it look right but I also had too many pieces left over. Then and only then do macho guys decide to read the directions. As a last resort. I could have saved hours of work if I had only read the directions first.

We have a tendency to do the same in our Christian walks. We attempt to do it all ourselves until we realize we're doing it wrong, going the wrong way, or messing up badly. Only then do we think to read God's directions. Doesn't it make good sense to read God's directions first, before we spend a good deal of our lives trying to correct the mistakes we made? We could have saved a lot of time, heartache, and misery if we'd only read and followed the instructions.

> *"Blessed is the man who walks not in the counsel of the ungodly, nor stands in the path of sinners, nor sits in the seat of the scornful. But his delight is in the law of the LORD; and in His law he meditates day and night. He shall be like a tree planted by the rivers of water, that brings forth its fruit in its season; whose leaf also shall not wither; and whatever he does shall prosper"* (Ps. 1:1–3).

It is hard to walk through a chicken coop without getting something unwanted on your feet.

I've heard many Christians say, "I will go to the clubs, bars, and anywhere the sinners go. How else can we win them to the Lord?" Is that a true and honorable mission from God or an excuse to go to the places sinners go? It's one thing to gain wisdom and knowledge and then be sent by God to go to those places to witness. But how often do those who make the above statement find themselves witnessing? If they aren't well grounded in the Word, instead of convincing the sinner to come to Christ, they conform to the ways of the sinner. God's Word wants us to win the sinner not by becoming one of them but by proving that they should become more like Jesus. If you are not read up and prayed up, you will get soiled. When you get soiled, your testimony gets soiled. We don't win the sinner by becoming one of them. If we become like them, we're proving to them that they don't need to change. They don't see a difference. If they don't see something better in a Christian, they will never want to become one. Or they are convinced they can be a Christian and still do the things they did before without changing. Unfortunately, the latter is what I see happening. There are many Christians claiming the title and still walking in the chicken coop. They become professing, not possessing, Christians smelly ones.

A young Christian doctor once asked me where he could find a young single Christian lady. He was a handsome man. He told me that he was a simple Christian who believed the Word of God for what it said. He said he adhered to old-fashioned values that never go out of style. He liked to open the car door for a lady, pay for the meal when they go out, and felt it important to get to know each other before getting serious. I told him what I believed to be true: the best place to find a good single Christian lady is in church. He told me he did go to a large church where there were many young ladies to choose from. He would date only ladies who claimed to have accepted Jesus as Savior. When he would go to open the door for them, they would look at him kind of strangely, and when the time came to pay for the meal, some wouldn't let him pay for theirs. After the second or third date, they asked him about moving in together. These are professing Christians.

It gets worse. Some were eager to have a baby with him and perfectly willing to have a child out of wedlock. As I looked into the church's preaching and teaching, I found that it taught that as Christians, we need to go where the sinners go. Walk with them and talk with them. When they see that you are just like them, they will want to come to your church. They also warned not to speak Scripture because it would chase them away. Don't ask them to accept Jesus because they would do that on their own. There is no place in Scripture where God tells Christians to become like the world. But the Bible does say that God commands Christians to invite sinners to become more like Christ (1 John 2:15–29; James 1:27).

> *"As for every man to whom God has given riches and wealth, and given him power to eat of it, to receive his heritage, and to rejoice in his labor; this is the gift of God" (Eccles. 5:19).*

God gives wealth as a gift for personal enjoyment.

> *"When you go you will come to a secure people and a large land. For God has given it unto your hands; a place where there is no lack of anything that is on the earth" (Judg. 18:10).*

A place where there is no want of anything that is in the earth a place of satisfaction with who we are and with what God has given.

> *"He that spared not his own Son, but delivered him up for us all, how shall he not with him also freely give us all things?"(Rom. 8:32).*

God looks for opportunities to bless us. We present those opportunities when we believe in Him by exercising faith.

> *"For I know the thoughts that I think toward you, says the LORD, thoughts of peace and not evil, to give you a future and a hope" (Jer. 29:11).*

The New International Version of the Bible translates the verse above as follows: *"'For I know the plans I have for you,' declares the LORD, 'plans to prosper you and not to harm you, plans to give you hope and a future.'"*

God not only wants us to prosper, He *plans* for us to prosper. It is up to us to follow His plan. Prosperity is a matter of holding on after others have let go. Giving up too soon is what causes so many to fall short of their goals. When we see others let go, it's easier for us to let go also. But that should make you more determined to hang on.

Rule 3: Be Thankful for What You Have

I once heard the Rev. Creflo Augustus Dollar Jr. say, "If your money is looking funny in your offerings, don't complain about it and ask, 'What's going on? Why aren't people giving?' Take what you have and thank God for what He has given you and don't complain about what you didn't get."

Thankfulness adds, and complaining divides.

One night a minister had a dream that he went on a tour of heaven. St. Peter met him at the gate to show him around. They came to a large room full of thousands of angels busily running back and forth.

"Why are they so busy?" the minister asked.

"This is the room where all the prayer requests from all over the world are received," St. Peter said. "The angels gather them all and prepare them for answers."

Next they came to another room, even larger than the first, where again there were thousands of angels running back and forth. The minister again asked what this room was that they all were so busy.

"This is the room where prayers from all over the world are answered," St. Peter said. "The angels are on duty 24-7."

Then they came to a small room with just one angel just standing there, waiting. The minister asked what this room was.

"This room is for those who took the time to thank the Lord for their answered prayer and show appreciation," St. Peter said.

> *"Blessed be the Lord, who daily loads us with benefits,*
> *The God of our salvation" (Ps. 68:19).*

God's gifts are never loans. They are always deposits. A loan is something we have to pay back, usually with interest. However, a gift is given for our use, without worrying about paying back.

The only people you should try to get even with are those trying to help you.

Too many people spend their days thinking of ways to get even with someone who has harmed them in some way. However, the time they spend trying to get even deprives them of the blessings they would have had if they had left the harm in God's hands and moved on in God's work. Think of the person you hate or despise. If you can truly pray for God's blessings and love to come into his or her life, you are removing a major roadblock that prevents God's blessings from flowing into our lives. When we can do this with a true heart, we are removing a major roadblock that may have been preventing God's blessing from flowing into our lives. (It is not our enemies that set the roadblocks in our hearts, it is us). It is also you and me that God has given power to remove those roadblocks with His help.

Rule 4: The Choice Is Ours

The choice is ours to keep it and be miserable or remove it and be blessed.

Happiness isn't having what you want but wanting what you have.

Not wanting what you have tells God you aren't happy with what He's already given you. To find God's blessings and happiness, you must first have a true want for what He's already given. God knows you'll never appreciate getting what you want if you don't appreciate what you already have.

The richest person in the world is the one who is content with what he has.

Appreciation is the beginning of blessing. Have you ever met someone who feels God owes them? They attempt to hold God's feet to the fire by saying that God's Word says that anything we ask in His name He will give. God doesn't owe us anything. If God did nothing for us for the rest of our lives, He's already given us much more than we deserve. If we got what we deserved, we wouldn't be going to heaven when we leave this earth. Jesus's death on the cross has eternal value that's worth more than anything the world has to offer.

While we are here, God allows us to take possession of what is His. That makes us stewards, not owners.

Outside of God's will, there can be no prosperity. In God's will, there can be no failure.

If prosperity is found in God's will, there can be no prosperity outside of His will. While you are in God's will, you trust Him completely. There can be no failure, although there may appear to be. God asks us to believe what we cannot see, not what we can see.

He who is not grateful for the good things he has would not be happy with what he wishes he had.

Thanking God for our blessings extends them. Failing to thank Him will soon end them.

"Be anxious for nothing; but in everything by prayer

and supplication, with thanksgiving, let your requests be made known to God" (Phil. 4:6).

Let God know you appreciate what He has already done.

Some people count their blessings on their fingers and their miseries on an adding machine. Did you ever talk to someone and ask them how they are? They will spend ten minutes telling you all their problems and miseries. They tell you what's going wrong instead of what's going right. Though it wasn't your intention, you gave them a reason to unload. But when they unload, it doesn't go away; they still have the load. The only difference now is that you have it also.

Which do you wish to hear? I'm sure you'd rather hear the good. Hearing good things gives us encouragement, while hearing the bad things causes discouragement in our own lives. Now, it's good to let people know about your illnesses so they can remember you in their prayers. If you don't tell them, they won't know your needs. However, you don't want to fall into the trap of letting your illnesses dominate your life. If you do, you'll be blinded to or will hinder the blessings God wants you to receive. If God's vision and blessings dominate your thinking, you leave yourself open for God to give you peace and happiness, even while you're dealing with your illnesses. Placing illness in God's hands brings healing.

There is one discouraging thing about the rules of prosperity: they won't work unless you do.

<u>Chapter 6 Action Project</u>

Say to yourself the following statements:

1. I will not blame God for my poverty.
2. I will not blame employer, state, government, or anybody for my poverty or lack.
3. I will not complain about what God has already given me.
4. I will thank God daily for what He has already given me.
5. I will show appreciation for what God has given me and has done for me.
6. I will remind myself daily that God wants me to prosper.
7. I will remove doubt from my mind that God can and will cause me to prosper.
8. I will follow God's instructions on His conditions for prosperity.

This week take a few minutes and send a note to those people who have reached out and greatly affected your life.

Also do this: reach out to help someone else get ahead.

Let your hopes, not your hurts, shape your future.
—Robert Schuler

Chapter 7: Take Action

"See, Father," said a small boy who was walking with his father by the river, "they are knocking the props away from under the bridge. What are they doing that for? Won't the bridge fall?"

"They are knocking them away," said the father, "that the timbers may rest more firmly upon the stone piers which are now finished."

God often takes away our earthly things that we may rest more firmly on Him.

—Choice Gleanings Calendar

What Are Our Props?

- Props are the reasoning or excuses we offer as to why we can't do something.
- Props are the worldly ways we keep in our lives as a backup just in case God fails to produce our desired results.

One year when I was young, I received a bicycle for Christmas, though I'd never ridden one. Luckily, it came with training wheels. The training wheels helped me keep my balance until I got accustomed to balancing on my own. When I was confident I was ready to ride on two wheels, it was time to remove the training wheels. The first ride was a wobbly one, and I wasn't certain I'd be able to balance the bike. Practice, though, increased my confidence, and I was able to go faster and faster. Eventually I was so confident that I set up a cinder block with a board and created a jump. The more I rode, the better I got. Wow! I was getting good so good that I demonstrated for my friends. After a few stitches and Band-Aids, I realized I wasn't cut out to be an Evel Knievel. Too much confidence in our own abilities can cause recklessness. But I realized that if I never took off the training wheels, I'd never be able to ride a bicycle.

Any time we do something for the first time, we're apprehensive, not knowing what's ahead. Some people are so apprehensive about trying something new that they never try. Others try and fail and stop trying. Either of the two situations deprives us of an abundance of excitement and blessings we would have received had we stuck with it until we were fluent. Rather than admit our own inadequacies or failures and keep on trying, we attempt to find something or someone to blame the failure on. As long as we can find something to blame our failures on, we will never grow beyond that point because

- it gives us an excuse not to try anymore;
- we remove ourselves from the guilt of failing; and
- it's easier accept defeat rather than improve our skills to achieve.

Back in my hometown of Tarrtown, Pennsylvania, there was a family that lived down the street from us. They lived close to the Allegheny River. They had one girl and eight boys. The parents wanted to try for their own baseball team with nine boys. In those days girls didn't play baseball. The next child was another girl. They tried again and finally achieved their worthy goal. The poor mother was with child every year of her young life.

Living along the river created some benefits as well as dangers. They had a boat they used for water skiing. By the age of five, all the children knew how to swim. One day, they were at the river, and the father put a life jacket on his smaller one and threw him out into the water. A shocked bystander asked, "What would you do if that child would drown?" He looked at her and without missing a beat said, "We'll just get another one next year."

The truth is that having many children and living close to the river poses a threat that one of the children might wander unnoticed to the river and accidentally fall into the water. If the child didn't know how to swim, it would mean sure death. The father had put a life jacket on the child and threw him into the water not because he didn't want him. He did it because he loved him. Knowing how to swim could someday save his life.

That is the way it is with our Lord. He throws us in or lets us get in deep water not to drown us but to teach us how to swim. He does this not because He doesn't care but because He loves us. As long as we can place blame on something or someone else for our problems, we will never overcome them. They will continue to haunt us by ruling our lives; we'll find ourselves slaves to the problem. Feelings of inadequacy, doubt, loss of confidence, and eventual depression often result.

How to Remove Our Props

We remove the props when we accept the responsibility for lack of accomplishment or failures by placing ourselves in God's hands. There may be someone who is trying to keep us from succeeding by throwing obstacles in our way and attempting every possible way to hold us back. Why would someone do that? Jealousy. People do not want to see anyone getting ahead where they themselves have failed or feel inadequate. As long as they can keep you behind them, they don't have to put forth any more effort to get ahead.

I have a great revelation for you: In everything we do, there is always someone who will attempt to stop us from succeeding. But we never become failures *until we let them*. It's easier to say "they won't let me," "they stopped me," or "I can't do [what I'm trying to do] because of someone else." It isn't *them* who caused you to fail. You failed because you let them and quit trying. It's easier to accept failure when we can blame someone else. As long as we find something or someone to blame, we'll go through life with training wheels.

We have to remove those props; otherwise, the props become our maximum standards. If we're going to have a prop, let it be the Word of God. Let that be our maximum standard. Within God's Word there is no maximum to our capabilities except what we impose ourselves. Remember, we fail many times at many things, but we never become a failure until we give up. It very well may be that somebody else placed a roadblock, or several roadblocks, in your way, and perhaps that person is truly responsible for your current condition or current failure. Now what you have is a roadblock to deal with. Removing it is your responsibility. It is how we deal with the roadblock that determines if we are going to grow. It is when we move on beyond the roadblocks that growth takes place and also brings our biggest blessings. It is our faith in God that gives us the spiritual eyes to see beyond the roadblock.

"If you have faith as a mustard seed, you will say unto this mountain, Remove from here to there; and it shall move; and nothing will be impossible for you" (Matt. 17:20b).

- If it doesn't move, go over it.
- If you can't go over it, go under it.
- If you can't go under it, go around it.
- If you can't move it, go under it, or go around it, stay and make it a gold mine.

Our God is bigger than any mountain in your life or mine. We are not alone. Is your God bigger than your mountain, or is your mountain bigger than your God? If the latter is the case, you're looking to the wrong god. However, in either case you are right. You see, getting to the other side is not the position you are in right now but a decision you make. You will be where you believe you will be or not be. We must look at our problems through God's eyes. Through His eyes we can see through the problem to the other side. On the other side lies an abundance of blessings. The bigger the problem, the bigger the blessings that await us beyond the mountain.

When David saw Goliath, he saw victory and not defeat, the solution and not the problem. Goliath was bigger than David, but God was bigger than Goliath. The eyes of the Israelite army saw a giant, but the eyes of God saw a midget. David knew this. God's plan for us always lies on the other side of a mountain. This may be a shocking revelation. When we search for God's will in our life, we first go to the Bible and read and pray. We ask God to open or close doors for us so we can know our direction. God does not seem to answer that prayer immediately or in the time frame that we expect. We must understand that God never opens a door wide enough for a train to go through. He just opens it a crack, and we are to push it open. When we come against resistance or meet an obstacle, we feel it must not be God's direction. We encounter those who are not willing to let us pass through the obstacles. It is then that so many of us give up and quit.

If we feel this way, we have to ask ourselves this question: why would God call us to a ministry if there were not obstacles to overcome? It just may be that He called us *because* of the obstacle or resistance. When we come to it, He may not remove it from our path, but He does promise to help us do so. If the door was wide open and there were no obstacles, you are going the wrong way. God wants us to move to the other side of the obstacle.

Getting to the other side requires action on our part. Many bystanders come to church for entertainment, to hear something that causes them to feel good, and to just watch the other workers. They go home and forget it until the next Sunday, thinking they have done their duty for God. They want to be seen as a good person because they go to church. They tell others they are Christians or that they are still searching for the truth. However, once you become a Christian and invite Christ into your life, you are no longer a bystander but a participant. No man comes to the Son unless called by the Father.

> *"And he said, Therefore, I have said to you, that no one can come to Me except it has been granted to him Father" (John 6:65).*

Make yourself available for God's use in the church. If you want to see your pastor have a heart attack, just go to him and ask, "What can I do for you or for the church?" Don't expect to be asked to do something you are already expert in. Be prepared to be asked to do something you've never done before. We are given opportunities to do for God. When you make yourself available to God, He will make Himself available to you. Your job is to step forward in faith.

> *"Draw near to God, and he will draw near to you"* > *(James 4:8a).*

For the next thirty days, pray the following: *God, what can I do for you? I want to make myself available.* Have you gotten into the habit of giving God your laundry list for the day? You tell

160

Him how you would like Him to help you in various situations. "Help me here, Lord," you pray. "Help me do this or that." I say *habit* because we sometimes lose sight of the fact that God is not our servant; we are His servants. A servant is one that does the bidding of the master.

We know God already knows our needs even before we ask. Should we not approach God with thanksgiving for what He has already given us? He tells us, "With thanksgiving let our requests be made known to him" (Phil. 4:6). Then ask Him the question, "Lord, what can I do for you today?" That is the heart of a servant.

We will have more prayers answered in one month when we ask God what we can do for Him than in one year continually asking Him to help us. Yes, we do need to bring our requests to Him, but our requests are secondary in importance to wanting to serve Him. He will place someone before you that is in need of your assistance, advice, or encouragement. He will also bring into your life those to help you along the road to prosperity.

Time to Take Action

You can know the Bible word for word. You can believe every word written. You can believe it applies to you. But it doesn't do anyone any good until you take action. This is where the tire meets the pavement. Taking action is actually applying God's Word to your everyday life situations. Action is the exercising of faith. God doesn't want us to just pray and then sit and wait for Him to do all the work. He expects us to get up on our feet and apply what we have learned. If applying what we've learned wasn't necessary, we could just go to school, graduate, and then retire for the rest of our lives. No, graduation is the beginning of our work, not the end.

Without action

- we cannot be useful to God;

- we cannot receive the blessings God wants us to have;
- we cannot be a blessing to others; and
- we cannot exercise our faith.

When we take action, we place ourselves between God and that with which He wants to bless us and use us to accomplish that mission. God can fulfill His promises in the Scripture only when we *take action*.

Take Action #1

We all need help from others at times, but the best helping hand you'll ever find is at the end of your arm. Everyone has his or her own life to live. Other people were not created just to help us reach our goals. If you need help doing something and wait for someone else to help you, you may wait a long time. Whatever you need done, just start it. Help will come much sooner, and you won't have to wait so long for completion.

Those who never take chances never make advances. Taking chances is a part of life. Many people do not take chances because of the fear of failure. They don't think far enough in advance to know that if they don't take the chance of failure, it is impossible to succeed.

The faith to move mountains always carries a pick. God says faith can move mountains. Faith, however, requires exercise. Exercise takes energy. Here is a mistake that many Christians make because they have not yet experienced the transformation from the worldly to the godly: they are so dependent on their physical surroundings that they attempt to move God with their minds, attempting to get Him to do things their way. That is attempting to move the spiritual with the physical. However, God does things just the opposite. He wants us to be submissive so He can move us with His Spirit.

When we try to move God, we always fail because we have

God working against us. He didn't call us to bring about our will in His life; He called us so He can bring about His will in our lives. When we let God move us, we are successful because we are willing to be moved by God. Faith keeps moving us forward, regardless of the obstacles that stand in our way. Most of the time that requires hard work.

Are you trying to move God, or are you letting God move you?

My wife, Laverne, can tell you that I am one who doesn't like to sit around and do nothing, even though there's a time when that's healthy. I have a saying that isn't entirely biblical, and I wouldn't recommend it for everyone: do something, even if it's wrong. This is in contrast to not taking any action or being unsure of what correct action to take. Putting your foot in the water is the only way of telling if God is going to part the sea before you.

All these things we do will soon pass, but only what we do for God will last. As we go through this life, we have to do things that soon will pass. However, where we should be concentrating most of our efforts is on doing things that will last. "What we do unto the least of these, we do it unto Jesus Himself" (Matt. 25:40).

A man without principles never draws much interest. There are many people in business who seemingly are getting ahead in this world by dishonest means. We look at them and wonder if that is not the best way to go. Just remember the above statement. Anything you achieve by dishonest means will never bring you peace, only disillusionment. Peace can never be found in dishonesty.

If you tell people what they want to hear, you think they will like you better and do as you ask. If you tell them the truth, you feel they will never follow you. But Christians don't lie or sugarcoat a lie. Sugarcoating is a lie just the same. "Satan is the father of lies, and the truth is not in him" (John 8:44).

If you are doing anything vocationally or in ministry

that cannot withstand the test of truth, it is not worth doing. Lies or deceit is not of God and cannot receive His blessings. The way of truth may take you longer, but when you arrive, you will have more and feel better about yourself and your accomplishments.

Take Action #2

Life is like a bank where you make deposits of what you wish to draw out at a future date. You can draw out only what you put in. None of us can expect to go down to our local bank and make a withdrawal of funds that we never put in. That is only common sense. Common sense seems to go by the wayside when it comes to the bank of life, though. We expect life to give us benefits that we never planted the seeds to achieve.

Don't expect a slap on the back until you start to work. Think of the fly. There are those who will not do anything unless they're sure they will get credit for it. Even if man doesn't see the work you do, God does. It is not man who does the rewarding but God. It is God who directs man. But we need to do something. "Faith without works is dead" (James 2:20).

Some people are not self-starters and have to be cranked before they move. There are people who will not budge unless they are prodded. They have a built-in excuse for failure. They justify lack of accomplishment by saying, "I did it only because I was asked" or "I did it only because they couldn't find anyone else." When they are prodded, they will quit before the work is complete. You have to keep checking on them to make sure they are doing their work and that it gets done.

As an employer, I tell my employees, "If I have to keep checking to see that you get done what is requested, then one of us is not needed. It takes double the time, double the money, and only half the work gets done." People who need to be cranked get highly irritated because you express dissatisfaction with their work and end up blaming you because you are "not a nice person." They don't care if work is done right or on time. Often you end up having to do most of the work they're supposed to do to begin with. These are ones you do not want to offer a raise or a promotion. They are unprofitable servants.

Self-starters, on the other hand, don't have to be prodded. They see work that needs to be done and do it. They usually make sure it's done on time and done right. These are the ones you offer raises and promotions. They are profitable servants. If you were God, which one's prayers would you be more ready to answer?

Start with what you can do and don't stop with what you can't do. Do your best, and God will do the rest. If you wait until you know it all before you start, nothing will ever get done. Start with what you have. Don't wait for what you want to have. Start from where you are and not where you want to be. Where you want to be is your destination. For some people, however, their destination is at the beginning. They never grow.

Those who deny themselves for Christ will enjoy themselves in Christ. God has placed this law into effect. We enjoy doing for others more than we enjoy doing for ourselves. When we put ourselves out for the Lord's use, we deny ourselves the time we would have spent for ourselves, but our rewards are more enjoyable and fulfilling.

Take Action #3

Always begin somewhere. You can't build a reputation on what you are going to do. People who are always talking about what they are going to do will probably not get anything done. Do something.

Don't think up a thousand reasons why you can't do something; just find one reason why you can. Does anyone like this come to mind when you present an idea? Even though he or she knows nothing about your idea, he or she will offer a thousand reasons why it cannot be done. This personality is self-defeating and self-destructive. People like this will never advance because of this attitude. Why would you think of a thousand reasons why something can't be done when all you have to do is think of one reason why it can? Being negative is hard work. There is nothing that cannot be done. It's not that it can't be done; it's just that some things take more time than others.

God calls men when they are busy; Satan calls them when they are idle. I have always worked long hours and days. When I was with a large insurance company for nineteen years, I worked sixty to seventy hours per week for at least thirteen of those years and used the weekends for work around the house. At the same time I was taking Bible classes to study for ministry work. I learned to make every minute count. There were times I couldn't get it all done myself and had to get help. Good work ethic learned early in life has helped me through hard times when they came and they did come in business, ministry, and family life.

If I really wanted something done, I asked someone who was already busy. A busy person will get more done than someone who has nothing to do. You see, the reason some people have nothing to do is because they don't want to do anything. Listening to them, you would think they are the hardest-working persons on earth. I learned long ago in my career that people will find reasons to do what they want to do and excuses to not do what they don't want to do. People with nothing to do are certainly not going to break their routine to do something for you. You can always depend on the busy person; you can never depend upon the person with nothing to do.

Don't die until you're dead. When I make this statement, people look at me strangely. Some people "died" many years ago; they just haven't gotten buried yet. You see, when we stop working or doing things, we speed up the dying process and aren't useful to our employers, our family, or anyone.

Keep on keeping on until you can't keep on anymore. Remember, if you try to go it alone, the fence that shuts others out shuts you in. There's a story of a man who built his house on top of a mountain. From his home he could see beautiful scenery in all directions. To the east was a lake, to the west were valleys, to the north was a forest, and to the south were hayfields. He decided to do some landscaping to spruce up the place. He put in shrubs close to the house, and around the outer property line, he planted trees for shade and a windbreak. As the years passed, the trees grew, and eventually he lost the beautiful view. Where there once has been a large world to see far away, he could now only see to the end of his yard. The wall of trees he had planted to protect himself from the elements had enclosed him in his own little world. He couldn't see the forest for the trees.

I've known people who have done the same thing in relationships with others. They got hurt in the past by a boyfriend, girlfriend, spouse, employer, friend, or someone else. The pain was so severe that they wanted to protect themselves from being hurt again. Assuming a new relationship would bring the same hurt, they built walls to keep others from getting too close and hurting them again. However, they found that the walls they built to keep others out became a prison, enclosing them in a very small world. They also limited their blessings to what was behind those walls. Do you ever find yourself doing the same thing? When you place your trust in our Lord, you don't need to build walls for protection. God will protect you.

God's Ways

> *"For My thoughts are not your thoughts, nor are your ways My ways, says the LORD. For as the heavens are higher than the earth, so are My ways higher than your ways, and my thoughts than your thoughts"* (Isa. 55:8–9).

God's ways are different than man's ways and are often the opposite of tradition.

> *"Making the word of God of no effect through your tradition which you have handed down" (Mark 7:13).*

Following the Lord's footsteps in the Bible, we find that He didn't follow tradition. He often did the opposite. Now, if God does not follow tradition, then we should also refrain from following tradition. Following our Lord means that we must be willing to break tradition.

I was in a discussion with a friend one time about a different interpretation of what the Bible said about a certain belief he was sharing, a belief I believed to be in error. He said, "Show me in Scripture." So I went home, got out my Bible, and accumulated more than twenty-eight verses that supported my view. I wrote them down for him to study and come to a conclusion. When I showed them to him, though, he threw the paper in the waste basket and said, "I don't care what you say. My grandfather was _____. My father and mother were _____, and I will always be _____." Upset that he didn't even look at the Scriptures I'd spent hours compiling, I looked him in the eye and asked, "If you were born in the back of a car, would you grow up to be a Buick?" You see, he wasn't shutting me out; he was shutting out the Word of God because he would sooner believe tradition than the Word of God.

We each have to answer for our own souls. Neither our grandparents nor our parents can save us. We need to seek God, not tradition. If they were right, the Scripture would bear that out. Yet we make the same choices every day, following worldly or supposedly religious traditions in place of the Word that Christ instructs us to follow. Tradition is much easier to follow and requires no effort. Tradition can destroy us; the Word of God saves us.

You can nullify God's Word in your life because of unbelief.

Unbelief destroys the effects of God's Word and keeps it from finding a home in our hearts, where our Lord wants to live.

Many people are willing to change not because they see the light but because they feel the heat. Have you ever read about criminals who took advantage of people in a dishonorable way for years and then finally got caught? At the trial they said how sorry they were for their dishonesty. They didn't want to go to jail. We have to ask, were they sorry for the wrong that they did to others, or were they just sorry for getting caught?

We as Christians can fall into the same trap. We have seen televangelists who have been blessed even though they were actually gaining wealth for dishonest pleasures. They thought they were getting away with these deeds because they were still being blessed financially. The sad thing is they showed no signs of repentance until they got caught. Did they repent because they really did not want to do the wrong or because they got caught? This is just one illustration that stands out. What about our everyday transactions with one another? Could we be guilty of the same?

There is nothing that escapes the eye of our Lord. Although we don't feel His wrath today, rest assured, we will—eventually. We cannot and will not get away with it. God, however, gives us room and time for true repentance. With God's all-seeing eye, we always get caught. But He gives us the opportunity to make it right. Don't wait until you feel the heat before you are willing to change.

Get Ready for Blessings

"Be not conformed to this world: but be ye transformed by the renewing of your mind, that ye may prove what is that good, and acceptable, and perfect, will of God" (Rom. 12:2).

(We learned this in our third lesson.)

> *"In all your ways acknowledge him and He shall direct your path" (Prov. 3:6).*

> *"I can do all things through Christ who strengthens me" (Phil. 4:13).*

> *"But seek first the kingdom of God and His righteousness; and all these things will be added to you" (Matt. 6:33).*

Remember, it's not what you have; it's what you do with what you have that makes all the difference. At the end of this life, God is not going to be impressed with what you have and neither will the undertaker. God is impressed only with what you do with what He has given you. That is what will make the biggest difference in your life, both here on earth and throughout eternity.

Chapter 7 Action Project

I will do the following:

1. Stop blaming my failures on someone else and realize that if I fail, it is my fault.
2. Take responsibility for what I say and do and not justify what I say or do by saying someone else caused me to do it.
3. Move beyond what I believe to be my physical, mental, or spiritual limit and trust God.
4. Ask God to remove all my props, and I will depend upon Him for my stability and success in life.
5. Recognize that God is bigger than any problem that can come my way.

Chapter 8: Tithe

In this chapter we'll begin with the foundation of financial blessings. It's an area in that answers directly the following age-old questions:

- Should I tithe on the gross or the net?
- I know the tithe was in the Old Testament, but is it in the New Testament?
- Where is God in my priorities?
- If I have to decide to pay bills or pay tithe, what should I do?
- Do we have to choose between God's tithe and worldly success?

These are all legitimate questions that will be answered by God Himself. I'm just quoting Him and testifying of His faithfulness when I follow His directions. I'll share many Scriptures with you to answer these questions and more. I'd like you to think about the importance of the tithe. In the book of Malachi, God poses a direct challenge:

> "Bring all the tithes into the storehouse, that there may
> be food in my house, and try me now in this, says the
> LORD of hosts, if I will not open for you the windows

of heaven, and pour out such blessings, that there will not be room enough to receive it" (3:10).

God is asking us to prove him in the tithe. When He asks us to test Him, we are the ones actually being tested. The tithe is a mirror that God asks us to hold up so we can look at our hearts to determine exactly where we place God in our lives. Many will be pleased with what they see, more will be shocked, but all of us will hang our heads when we realize what our God has done for us and how little we do for Him. Read on with an open mind.

Give From What You Have

A minister said to a new convert in a mission chapel in Cuba, "Cristobel, if you had a hundred sheep, would you give ten to the church?"

"Yes, I would," the farmer answered.

"Would you do the same for a hundred cows?" the minister asked.

"Yes, I would."

"Would you for a hundred horses?" the minister persisted.

"Yes, of course I would," the farmer answered.

"If you had ten pigs, would you give one of them to the Lord?" the minister asked.

"No, I wouldn't, and you have no right to ask me that, preacher," the farmer said. "You know I have ten pigs."

It is easy to give what we don't have. Once we have something, it requires faith to give it up.

"For if there be first a willing mind, it is accepted according to what one has, and not according to what he does not have" (2 Cor. 8:12).

God's Word reminds us of His credentials: how He brought the world into existence, how He delivered the children of Israel from hundreds of years of bondage and brought them to the promised land, how He fed them in the wilderness and brought them water from a rock. He tells us how He gave His only Son, Jesus, to die on the cross, be resurrected on the third day, and ascend to the Father. He reminds us how He sent the Holy Ghost to live within us, how the Holy Spirit is our personal mentor, and how the Word of God is our guide through life. We can receive all the blessings of His promises if we just follow His directions to the tee. If we do, He will guarantee prosperity. Listening to God will lead to eternal life and no limits.

Do we have to choose between God and worldly success? This is a question we all deal with every day of our lives. The answer is no. We do, however, choose which one is the master and which is the servant. You choose which one you place first before anything or anyone. That choice determines where your heart is. We can know God and be successful entrepreneurs. Worldly success places money before God, and all those who place worldly success before God have to show for it is their money, expensive toys, and loneliness. They still feel an emptiness that things cannot fill. Christian success, on the other hand, places God before money. In the end, they can all have the same as non–Christians, but they also possess happiness and a peace beyond understanding that fills the void we all search to fill. Inner peace, true happiness, and eternal life are things God provides that the world cannot.

This is the choice we make every Sunday morning:

- To tithe or not to tithe? If we tithe, how much?
- To tithe from the gross or the net?
- To pay man first or God?

Hopefully by now you are able to hold up this spiritual mirror and see exactly where your heart is. By the way, where is your heart? If you don't quite know yet, in this session you will see exactly where it is. If you find it is not where it should be, then you'll need to make a decision to conform to the world or to Jesus. If you want to conform to Jesus, you need to follow His direction, which is set forth in His Word.

Purpose of the Tithe

> *"Honor the LORD with your possessions, and with the first fruits of all your increase; So your barns will be filled with plenty, and your vats will overflow with new wine"* (Prov. 3:9–10).

Giving God the first of all is showing God honor. When you implement a divine principle, you will reap a divine reward. You cannot receive divine supplies when you violate the divine principle of the tithe and the first fruit.

When first things are put first, the second things are not suppressed but increased. When a seed is planted in the ground, it has to first die and then the fruit comes. Before the seed can grow up, it must first grow down and develop roots to give a solid foundation that provides support for the growth and fruit. The first fruit is holy, and if the root is holy, then the whole vine and fruit are holy. If the root is corrupt, then the whole vine is corrupt.

If you first determine whether your employer is going to offer you a raise or cut your pay or if you evaluate what the market is going to do before you plant the first fruit in God's garden, you are confirming your faith to be in the physical that you see and not in the God that you cannot see, and thus you lack belief in Him. That lack of belief that violates God's principles.

Ecclesiastes 11:4 says, "He who observes the wind shall not sow; and he who regards the clouds will not reap." In other words, those who wait for all conditions to be favorable before they proceed will not sow or reap.

*"Will a man rob God? Yet you have robbed me, But
you say, in what way have we robbed You? In tithes
and offerings. Ye are cursed with a curse: for you have
robbed Me, even this whole nation. Bring all the tithes
into the storehouse, that there may be food in My house,
and try Me now with this, says the LORD of hosts, if
I will not open for you the windows of heaven, and pour
out for you such blessings, that there will not be room
enough to receive it"* (Mal. 3:8–10).

Our finances are under a blessing if we tithe. We will receive
peace and satisfaction, and God will open the gates of heaven
and pour out blessings we will not have room to receive. Our
finances are under a curse if we withhold. What part of our tithe
we do not give back to God will never bring us any peace and
satisfaction, only misery.

God left the choice in our hands to decide whether we
want our finances under His blessings or under His curse. If
we decide not to tithe, they are under a curse. Being under a
curse means that God has withdrawn His blessings from your
finances.

Christians are fooling themselves by justifying reasons for
not tithing and then asking God to bless their finances. We
cannot refuse to follow God's direction and expect Him to
fulfill His promise. Understand this: *it is impossible to receive the
blessings this verse promises without tithing.* If we don't have the faith
to tithe, how can we have the faith that God will go against
His Word to answer our prayer for financial deliverance? By
refusing to tithe, you have doubted Him.

I wish I could say that this illustration is an exception to the
rule; however, there are many Christians hurting and getting in
deeper and deeper in debt, and they can't understand why God
doesn't deliver them. The answer is not because God doesn't
love them or care. It is because they don't believe God when
he says, "Bring your tithe into my storehouse and see if I don't

open up the windows of heaven and pour out blessing that you will not have room to receive." If you are really serious about being delivered, you need to start tithing.

> *"On the first day of the week let each of you lay something aside, storing up as he may prosper that there be no collections when I come" (1 Cor.16:2).*

The first day of the week is Sunday. Or would we rather wait until we are sure we have enough money to pay our bills to determine if we have enough left to tithe? In the appendix at the back of this book are a few testimonies of those who have been through my seminar on Christian prosperity. Some were paying all their bills first, and then at the end of the week, they would determine the tithe. With that concept they found themselves in financial despair. When they completed this study and started paying their tithe at the first of the week, they saw the promises of God coming to pass in their lives just as God promises. He will do the same for you.

> *"And if you are Christ's, then you are Abraham's seed, and heirs according to the promise" (Gal. 3:29).*

God blessed Abraham's seed as the sands of the sea. Let us look at Abraham's seed not as physical seed but spiritual seed—the seed of faith. God has preserved a bloodline of the faithful from which Jesus was born, and it is through Jesus that the nations of the earth have been blessed.

Old Testament/New Testament

> *"Woe to you, scribes and Pharisees, hypocrites! For you pay tithe of mint and anise and cumin, and have neglected the weightier matters of the law, justice and mercy and faith: these you ought to have done, without leaving the others undone" (Matt. 23:23).*

Note, don't leave the tithe undone.

"You shall have no other gods before Me" (Exod. 20:3).

That includes the god of money. If we place our money before God, we worship our money; we have more faith and confidence in money than God's promise. God cannot bless that area of our lives. You may say, "I don't place my money before God." However, when it comes time to give God His portion or use it for ourselves, what are we doing? This is something Christians do all the time without even realizing it. We need to make a conscious effort to put God first in our lives, which includes our money. We are all creatures of habit. We develop good habits and bad habits. Bad habits are easier to develop and come naturally. Good habits we have to work at. When we acquire the habit of putting God first, only then will we realize the fruit of Malachi.

A blessing that is shared is not halved but doubled. This is a comparison of the natural law and the spiritual law. The natural law states that if you share something with someone else, you lose the part you shared. The spiritual law states that what you share is doubled. Many of us refrain from sharing because we think in terms of loss. If I share, then I won't have. God, however, says differently. Which law do you believe?

If someone loses his or her temper, does that mean he or she doesn't have it anymore? When he or she shares his or her temper, it doesn't go away but is now enjoyed by all within hearing distance, especially the one it is directed against. Now, if this person gives his or her temper to you, he or she shouldn't have it anymore, correct? Wrong. The more that person exercises it, the more he or she has it. So it is with faith.

An Act of Faith

"And he sought God in the days of Zechariah, who had understanding in the visions of God: and as long as he sought the LORD, God made him to prosper" (2 Chron. 26:5). This verse speaks of Uzziah, who succeeded his father Amaziah. Uzziah was sixteen when he was made king, and then he reigned for fifty-two years.

As long as he sought the Lord, God made him to prosper. The key is seeking the Lord. If we don't keep Him first, we will be in want. If we put our problems or our money before God, we will always be in want. It is impossible to prosper under God's system of prosperity without tithing.

We don't tithe because we feel we have to but because we trust God and want to honor him. This is the reason for tithing not because we need something but because we wish to honor God. If we honor God with our tithe, He is faithful to reward the giver. Remember, God owns everything; we own nothing. Whatever we have, it is not ours. It belongs to God.

I have heard it said that sinners get ahead accumulating wealth, and they don't tithe. God has meant His wealth for the Christian. When God's people refuse to trust Him and tithe, He offers what is meant for God's people to the sinner. However, the sinner's increase brings the curse instead of the Christian's blessing.

"Now He did not do many mighty works there because of their unbelief" (Matt. 13:58).

Belief in Christ causes Him to do mighty works. Where there is unbelief, there are no works.

Let's look at what Jesus says about works of Believers and unbelievers

First Fruit

First fruit is giving off the top before taxes and deductions.

The first fruit is the first that appears on the plant first ear of corn, first berry, first apple, first dollar. First fruit is not what we put in our pockets after deductions. If that were the case, we could also include our mortgages, electric bills, car payments, loans, and all our bills as deductions. What then would be left to tithe from? The real question is where you place God in your life, business, and home. We do not place Him first if we put our government, state, and local taxes before Him.

In the Old Testament, they paid taxes but gave of the first fruit. They didn't have the convenience of payroll deductions. If we give back to God after deductions, anything we place before God cannot be under His blessing but under the curse. We attempt to make ourselves feel good by saying we don't put it all in our pocket. That sounds good if we believe our own deceit. On the other hand, if we truly believe that God is true to His Word and gives back, we would have no problem giving off the top because we would know that God always gives back more than we give. He will not be indebted to us. When we give off the top, God will bless the purpose of the gift and the giver all the more.

God's Adding Machine

If we truly believe that all comes from God, then tithing is not a loss of 10 percent but a gain of 90 percent. Our carnal thinking makes us ask, "If I can't pay bills now with 100 percent, how am I possibly going to pay them with 90 percent?" We're using an adding machine made by man. If we give the 10 percent, the 90 percent that's left will do more than the 100 percent would have. When you use God's adding machine, $100 minus $10 equals $100 plus. Which adding machine do you use? If you are not using God's than you need to change adding machines. God's ways are always different than man's ways.

> *"For My thoughts are not your thoughts, nor are your ways My ways, says the LORD. For as the heavens are higher than the earth, so are My ways higher than your ways, and My thoughts higher than your thoughts"* *(Isa. 55:8–9).*

The most difficult thing people have to give is their money. Whatever is closest to a person's heart is the most difficult to give up. Unfortunately, for most people it is their money. Relationships with spouse, family, church, and God are laid at the altar of sacrifice because of the love of money.

- We must release before we can receive.
- We can't expect God to do the last part of Malachi 3:10 until we do the first part.
- A carnal mind cannot grasp the concept of tithing.
- Put Him first and then trust Him for your needs.
- The tithe is not our money. It belongs to God. He gives us 100 percent. We give Him 10 percent and keep 90 percent.

Our main problem is that we treat the money God gives us as ours, with the attitude that "I worked for it, and it's mine." If we truly know that it belongs to God, then we have the better end of the bargain: we keep 90 percent. What if God would ask for the 90 percent and ask us to keep the 10 percent? This wouldn't mean we would have less but that God would have more to bless us with. How can you lose?

Do you ever pray, "God, give me more, and I will tithe"? I'm sure we're all guilty of that prayer. This is worldly thinking. We're dictating to God how we'll accept His Word. We're wanting God to be our servant instead of us being servants of God. We're so used to making the rules that we try to get away with it with God. He doesn't work that way. If you negotiate with your employer for a $50 raise in salary and he agrees, why would you continue to negotiate? Why would you negotiate with God for something He has already given?

Can we really say that God is first in our lives and then put money ahead of Him by not giving Him the first 10 percent? Can God really be first in all *but* our money? Can we believe without doubt that our prayers will be answered if we have already doubted God in our tithe?

It takes faith to give off the top. It doesn't take faith to give the leftovers. Are we guilty of giving God the crumbs that fall from our table? This is exactly what we're doing when we take care of all our needs and then give to God what we don't need for our own living. Remember the rich man and Lazarus. The rich man consumed until he was full and gave Lazarus the crumbs that fell from his table. When we attempt to justify to God why we don't tithe, stating it's our duty to take care of our families, pay bills, put food on the table, and do those things first, are we giving God the crumbs that fall from our tables? Do we really think God will let our families starve if we give to Him first?

Have you ever been around people who, if you took the word *I* out of their vocabulary, would be speechless? Using the word *I* is crediting ourselves. We have achieved or given because of our own power or ability. Do you like to be around someone who is constantly bragging? Neither does God.

Testimonies

J.C. Penny tithed 90 percent of his income and built his financial empire on the 10 percent he kept for himself. Those who fall short attempt to make excuses why someone else has greater achievements. This makes them look better. When I've shared the story of J.C. Penny, the first thing people say is, "He could give because of his success." Or was he successful because he gave?

John D. Rockefeller, who built the Rockefeller empire

with Standard Oil, had a monopoly in the oil industry. At that time, monopolies were not illegal. In his will, he left his empire to his son, John Jr., with one condition that he tithe his income to the church. (He gave not only 10 percent to the church but also gave to notable charities, giving in the neighborhood of 35 percent). David Rockefeller also followed this practice.

Christian author **Jack Hartman** was facing bankruptcy when business took a tumble. His wife asked him if they should give less to the church in order to pay business bills. He said, "No. *Increase* the tithe." This is faith in action. He increased at a time when all logic said differently. God honored his faith, and he prospered abundantly. His goal is to give 90 percent of his income. He testifies that it's much easier to give 15 percent than it is to give 10 percent and much easier to give 20 percent than 15 percent. This testimony came *after* he had increased giving by those percentages.

Jack Hartman has been an inspiration to me. His book, *Trust God for Your Finances*, encouraged me through financial hard times. I would have thought he would retire now that he's in his midseventies, but he's in Florida, working harder than ever. He publishes through Lamplight Ministries and sends books and literature all over the world to third-world countries, prisons, and the needy. This is quite an undertaking. I asked him what he charges for them. His response was shocking to me. He charges nothing. He gives away 80 percent of his literature. I asked him how he manages with expenses for his publications. He said that money just comes from areas and places that are not always of his understanding.

Do these men give because they have, or do they have because they give? Christians who lack faith, who refuse to trust God in their giving, use many reasons (excuses) for not giving. They are the ones who state, "Others give because they have." (In other words, they have to see it before they will believe it.)

If they accept these excuses, they will never have abundance and will always be in want.

Bob Morris says he counseled hundreds in the area of finances. He asked all of them the same question: Do you tithe? If not, why? If so, do you find yourself in want? The ones who tithed said they were blessed because of it. The ones who didn't said they couldn't afford to tithe; their finances were in shambles, or they were in want.

Bob, an evangelist, and his wife, Debbie, had been living from week to week for years. They both have giving hearts and gave away twelve of their automobiles and four homes. One night he gave their car to someone in need and the same night gave away their home. Bob testifies that as he sat on his rocking chair, thinking, *Now what? I don't have a place to live and no transportation.* The very next day God had miraculously provided both for them.

He now pastors the Gateway Church in South Lake, Texas, between Dallas and Fort Worth. He accepted the pastorate in 2000 with a church of 225. In a short time they built a $15 million church. The day the church was dedicated was the day they made the last payment. Instant growth led to a $5 million addition. Before it was complete, they had to call people and tell them to stop sending money. It was already paid for. He now has a congregation of 15,000, which has purchased property for another expansion. I recommend picking up his book, *The Blessed Life.*

I had the opportunity to visit his church. Until then, I thought such growth was due to watered-down preaching. My wife and I found out differently: Bob preaches the Bible and sound doctrine. Back home, when we testified to the success of a man faithful to God in his giving, the response was almost unanimous: his success was because he was near Dallas, where there's wealth.

Why is it that even the strongest of Christians cannot believe

God is faithful to His Word, and He doesn't need the wealth of man to bless His children? They doubt God as being able. That attitude is a reflection of many Christians who limit their own potential. I would rather believe that God is faithful to the faithful. That is why this subject of prosperity must be taught. It seems even Christians we look up to lack faith. People who don't tithe may have a lot of money, but it will never bring them satisfaction.

I've been a hunter all my life. I never was the brightest light bulb on the Christmas tree, but I do know that if I never aimed at a deer, I'll never have a chance of hitting one. God gives us visions, translated in our terms as goals—His goals for us. Aiming is a concentrated effort of focusing on that goal. If we blink our eyes or get sidetracked, we won't be able to hit it. Is it guaranteed that we will hit it? Perhaps not, but the only chance we have is to aim at the target.

Farmers Bring in the Tithes

The First Baptist Church in Abernathy, Texas, has five hundred members. Most of the adult men are farmers on the rolling plains around Abernathy, a town of 1,692 in west Texas, north of Lubbock. One spring many years ago, their pastor, C.A. Kennedy, age 35, asked them to dedicate one-tenth of their land to God and see what the returns would be. That year their tithes filled two washtubs with $14,132.65 in cash and checks, money from the harvest on the land they dedicated to God in the spring. Albert Hart dedicated five acres. Late in the summer he called the pastor to his farm to show him his acreage. All was bountiful, but on the dedicated land, the cotton stood twelve inches higher than the rest and yielded one and a third bales an acre compared with an average yield of one bale an acre on his other land.

"Bring all the tithes into the storehouse, that there may

*be food in My house, and try Me now in this, says the
LORD of hosts, if I will not open for you the windows
of heaven, and pour for you such blessing, that there will
not be room enough to receive it" (Mal. 3:10).*

Every word of action is a seed sown and will produce the
fruit according to the type of seed sown.

Remember, the more you lose your temper, the more
you have it. Once again I ask, have you ever been around
anyone who lost his or her temper? Do you know someone
who consistently loses his or her temper? Do you avoid being
around that person? The answer for most is yes. When a person
loses his or her temper, it has a negative effect on everyone
around that person. Losing your temper doesn't mean it's gone
forever just the opposite. It's like exercising: the more you do,
the easier it gets.

The same effect occurs with good things you do. The more
you do, the more you want to do. The good has a positive effect
on those around you, and people like to be around people who
have a positive effect on them, even if they don't admit it. What
we practice or exercise the most is in areas of our lives in which
we want to become stronger. So the question is, do you wish
to have a positive effect on yourself and those around you or a
negative one?

If your answer is positive, you must have some type of
control or restraint on the negative so that the positive can
be released. The negative influences cause negative actions in
our lives and will prevent the positive from existing, even if
our desire is to do otherwise. I've heard people say, "I can't
help it. It just comes out." Remember, "Legion" that Jesus was
confronted with in the book of Luke?

*"For he had commanded the unclean spirit to come out
of the man. For it had often seized him, and he was
kept under guard, bound with chains and shackles; and*

he broke the bonds, and was driven by the demon into the wilderness" (Luke 8:29).

This man was bound by man and Satan. The chains man had put on him were broken by the strength of the man; however, the bands of Satan he could not break without Jesus. Only Jesus could free him. Before he would listen to Jesus and follow Him, he had to be loosed from Satan.

"For which I suffer trouble as an evil doer, even to the point of chains; but the word of God is not chained" (2 Tim. 2:9).

There are bonds we willingly put on ourselves, even if we know they will be destructive to us. The Word is not bound. Jesus has the power to free you. It comes down to a choice. Do you want to stay in the bonds or be free? We seem to try everything the world has to offer for that freedom and keep falling short, when all the time freedom was just a prayer away. We need to condition ourselves to call upon Jesus when we're dealing with a temper or a destructive habit. If you have a temper out of control and decide to keep it, you are keeping it because you want to and not because you have to. But please don't share it with others. When I make this statement, I get a lot of raised eyebrows. But think about it:

- Does God really multiply what you have? No, that is our reward to use for ourselves.
- Does God multiply what you withhold? No, we withhold because we doubt and God does not reward doubt. Jesus says that He will multiply what you give and divide what you withhold.

To our carnal way of thinking, if we withhold, we'll have enough to do what we want. But that will multiply our problems, not our opportunities. Remember, what you withhold will be divided. What this all means is that the decision to tithe or not tithe has nothing to do with how much money you have or how many bills you have. Tithing is a demonstration of our belief in God's Word and trusts Him to keep His Word. The tithe is the mirror to our souls that demonstrates where we place God on our priority list. I encourage from this day forward that you lay all your excuses for not tithing on the altar of sacrifice and not lay your faith in God on the altar of sacrifice. *You can trust God. Give God your first and trust Him for the rest.*

Chapter 8 Action Project

I will do the following:

1. Remember the first 10 percent of my income belongs to God.
2. Place God before my money.
3. Place God before my bills and trust God.
4. Tithe 10 percent of my earnings.
5. Know that if I use that 10 percent for myself, whatever I use it for will not prosper.
6. Remember that God's work and ministry are more important than my own needs.

Chapter 9: Gifts and Offerings

ONE day when my son, Scott, was in high school, he came to me and asked, "Dad, when I graduate, can I do what I want to do or do I have to go to college?" When I asked him what he wanted to do, he said he wanted to be a truck driver. Not to be demeaning of a profession, I told him, "Son, if you wanted to be a refuge collector or a janitor, then that is what you need to be doing. But whatever you decide, learn the job, work hard at it, and do the best you can. Being your best at what you do puts you in demand, and employers will be looking for you. No employer wants an employee without initiative; however, every employer looks for those who are good at what they do and have a heart for their work."

I knew several truck drivers, and none of them really loved what they were doing. I believed that once the novelty wore off, truck driving would become more like work. So I asked Scott to talk to truck drivers that were actually driving for a living before making his final decision. He did so and changed his mind. Truck driving is hard work.

Determining what to do with your life is a major decision that we all face. Too many people go through life without making that decision, just bouncing from job to job. I've heard many students say they are looking for the highest paying job they were capable of doing. When I asked if they would enjoy it, the response was, "No, but I need the money to do the things I want to do in life." That is master disaster thinking.

Your vocation is something you will normally work at eight hours a day, five days a week, fifty-two weeks a year for forty-five years or more. If you do that just for the money, you are going to torture yourself for the rest of your life. You see, you are binding yourself to a negative. When you have a negative in your life, it affects everyone around you. It affects your spouse, your children, the people you socialize with, and your employer, as well as your job performance. You will earn every dime of your paycheck.

So if you want to enjoy life and have a positive effect on your life and those around you, find something you love to do. Then you'll enjoy your work so much that it won't seem like work. You'll be getting paid for doing what you love. When you enjoy it, you'll want to learn everything you possibly can about it, train yourself to do the best job you can. In doing so, you'll become in demand to employers. Those in most demand also get the most pay for their positions. Even if you don't get the highest pay, it's better to be doing something you enjoy and be happy than to have a well-paying job and be miserable for forty-five years.

Now I'm going to add one more factor into that decision. Knowing our Lord knows more about us, what is best for us, and what we'll be happier with, doesn't it make sense to go to Him for direction? He'll never guide us in a way that will harm us. Whatever way He guides us, we will find happiness. It may not be the easiest route, but it will be the one that brings us the most joy and fulfillment.

Generally, those who don't enjoy their work are more reluctant to give of what they've earned. That's because getting it is such a rigorous routine. Those who do enjoy their work are more willing to share. God uses our vocations as a means to channel His wealth to us and to His work.

Gifts

There's a difference between the tithe, an offering, and a gift. All of our income belongs to God but he requires the tithe of 10% to be returned to Him; we return it to Him, and He leaves us with the rest. If we give to other causes outside our tithe, we're giving money that belongs to God, not us. The tithe goes to the storehouse. An offering or a gift starts where the tithe leaves off. What we give out of what is left after the tithe is ours to give as a need arises or for a specific cause.

If you see a need and give to that need, this is a *gift* and is usually a one-time event.

An *offering* is similar to gift. A need is brought to your attention for a cause, and you give to that cause. Unlike a gift, which is a one-time event, an offering may be ongoing. Both come under the category of giving.

> *"Give, and it shall be given to you; good measure, pressed down, shaken together, and running over, will be put into your bosom. For with the same measure that you use, it will be measured back to you"* (Luke 6:38).

The giving comes first. As mentioned in a previous chapter, we seem to want to make deals with God on this one. We say, "God, you give to me, and then I'll have more to give to You." We don't believe God will fulfill His share of the bargain. We try to set the rules for God to follow so we cannot lose. (God doesn't work that way, though.) It's when we exercise faith in God by giving that brings into action God's part of returning.

It shall be given unto you again. There is no room for a *may* or a *might* be given. God says *shall*.

Good measure, pressed down, and shaken together and running over—this means that God will always give back more than we give. You cannot outgive God. Just try.

In Malachi 3:10, God challenges us to test Him: *"Bring into the storehouse and see if He will not open up the heavens and pour out blessings that we will not have room to store."* This is a test of faith. When we accept the challenge, we believe God will follow through with His promise. Also, by accepting it we prove to ourselves that God is more important in our lives than our money, that He is the provider, and that we cannot outgive God.

Shall men give unto you—God will cause men to give to you. You need not be concerned where it's going to come from. Notice there is nowhere in Scripture where God uses the person to whom we give as the one to return. There are those who don't give freely because they think the person to whom they're giving will never be able to repay them financially or return a like favor if they have a need. God never asked us to give only if we could see where or how we would get it back. Just the opposite. We are to give as though we're giving to Jesus and release it. Those to whom we give have to look into their own spiritual mirrors, just as we do.

"He who has a generous eye will be blessed; for he gives of his bread to the poor" (Prov. 22:9). The gift is given to those who will not be able to pay it back.

The ultimate accountant is God. Who goes go to an accountant he doesn't trust? Nobody. Why would you have someone you don't trust handle your financial affairs? You'd always be wondering if you're going to get ripped off. When it comes right down to it, that's the only reason we don't give freely. We don't trust God with our money. We're so afraid that we're going to lose it, that He will not give it back as He promised. Whom do you trust? Do you trust your own ability to prosper with it, or do you trust God?

> *"So let each one give as he purposes in his heart, not grudgingly, or of necessity, for God loves a cheerful giver" (2 Cor. 9:7).*

God knows if a pry bar is needed to cause you to give. When you give, He knows the attitude of your heart—either resentment or love. A gift means that you let go after you give. Do you know people whose gifts have a rubber band attached? They give, but they hang on and don't really want to let go. I do want to qualify this. We want to be careful where and to whom we give. If you give where it is ill-used and not for the purpose of God, it's not a good thing. It is feeding the problem.

> *"Do not give what is Holy to the dogs, nor cast your pearls before swine, lest they trample them under their feet, and turn and tear you in pieces" (Matt.7:6).*

If you know your gift will be misused to further someone's sinful habits, you're doing more damage than good. You're encouraging that person's bad habits and enabling instead of helping him or her to destroy the habit. If you give a gift for a certain need and that person then uses his or her own money to perpetuate the habit, what then? When we know our gift helps to destroy someone's initiative to combat a habit, it can become wrong to give. We think we're doing good, but we are causing further harm. As long as that person can count on your generosity, he or she can keep his or her bad habits.

I know this can be a struggle. Laverne and I have this situation with those close to us to whom we want to reach out; however, by giving to them we'd be enabling their continued harm to themselves. So we pray, witness, and attempt to lead them to the Giver of Life, Jesus. Will God still follow through with His promise to us if we do so? Yes. God encourages us to give and will not go back on His promise to us if our gifts are ill-used. He will bless us, but the one who uses them wrongly will not receive fulfillment but further abuse. As I said before, they have to look in their spiritual mirrors, and so do we.

If God owns all, we need to ask what He wants done with His property.

Do you think God would want His property used for satanic or destructive purposes? When I say destructive, I mean used for a message that destroys character or spiritual well-being or leads someone away from Christ. Whenever possible, research to make sure the cause you're giving to is using the gift for the purpose God laid on your heart when you decided to give. There are other times when God lays upon your heart the need to give to a person in the course of your daily life. Ask God to direct you to someone with a need with which you may be able to help, and He will bring that person across your path.

Laverne and I give to many causes. We have been giving mostly to nonprofit organizations. We, in turn, can benefit with a tax write-off. If there is a need in an area for which we cannot get a write-off, it doesn't stop us from giving. We don't give because of the write-off. That's just an added perk. Being a good steward of your gift is dependent upon the need being met, not the tax implications. When we get a refund, we have more to give. Many of the areas to which we give, which God has laid on our hearts, have never responded with a receipt or thanks.

We approach God in our prayers offering Him thanks for what He has already given us. For those that appeal for donations should approach those giving with thanks for what they have already received and then make request for additional funding. By showing appreciation for what we already received will open the door for God and others to give more. Lack of appreciation stops the stream.

Listen, God wants us to come to Him and make our requests with thanksgiving. If we are not thankful for what God has already given, why should He give us more? We feel the same way. We go into churches as visitors and give to the needs of that church. We look for areas where they are stepping out on faith and using God's funds for the Kingdom. We know our gift will be used. This statement may need qualification. There are many ministries out there. God wants His church to be ministering to the lost and needy. He wants us giving to a cause that will use our gift, not squander it. Giving is an act of faith, and faith is what He honors. Doesn't it make sense that He wants us giving to a ministry where they are stepping out on faith?

When Laverne and I give to a cause, a good indicator that it is needed or appreciated is if we receive a simple receipt with a note of appreciation. I want to clarify that we never give for the thanks, but the thanks is a strong indicator of the need and that the gift is being used for God's purpose. We are then encouraged to give more. When we receive nothing from a church or organization in acknowledgment of receipt or appreciation, it's an indication that it was not needed or appreciated. No response is sending a message that it didn't mean anything to them. We no longer send gifts there. It's like they're saying it wasn't important to them. Gifts are always important to those with needs. A simple thank-you goes a long way for future gifts.

Facts About Giving

Do you need to see where it's going to come from before you give? Do you say, "My income is limited, and my employer/ state/government/ won't give me more," and think that God can't give back because of your unique situation? Do you really think God needs your employer, the state, or the government for you to be able to give? Does He need their money, or does He have enough of His own?

The answer is simple, but many of us actually think that our money comes from these areas and that God cannot bless us without them. Just because we cannot see where or how God is going to bless us does not mean He can't. He is God. He can distribute those funds only when we exercise our faith, so we are blessed according to our own faith.

If we give according to our means, we wouldn't act mean when asked to give.

Have you ever asked someone to give to a cause, and the person's response was a mean remark such as, "They're always asking for money. Money, money, money! They must think we're made of it." How does that make you feel? Does it discourage you? It may make you apprehensive to ask anyone else. Let me put you at ease. God does not need that person's money. People who respond like that are not giving according to their means. They struggle parting with that with which God has blessed them. Pray for them but move on to the next potential giver.

Joy comes from giving, not getting.

Those who give reluctantly do not enjoy giving. This is because they feel that parting with something of their own will cause loss. If they give, they won't have enough to do what they want to do for themselves. You can just see their eyes not wanting to leave the dollar as it passes into the hands of another, like they just lost their best friend. Yet there are others who give with a smile. You can just see the joy in their hearts. God's true believers find the joy in giving more so than getting.

He who gives when he is asked has already waited too long.

We need to have our spiritual eyes trained to see a need before it is presented. I know that sometimes that's difficult to interpret. Some people don't want others to know their needs and are embarrassed about their condition. That's why our spiritual eyes need training. How do we train them? Mostly by prayer for God's direction.

There's a difference in being moved by the world and being moved by God. We look for ways and seek to be moved by God. However, we must be on guard, for the world wants to move us away from God to the world. When God's will is at stake, we must be strong enough to withstand the strength of worldly allurements. An old graveyard headstone reads:

What I spent I had.

What I saved I lost.

What I gave I have.

Just what does that mean?

- What you spent is gone, and you will never see it again. You probably can't remember where it went.
- What you had saved stays behind. You cannot take it with you to heaven.
- What you give is the only thing you will take with you when you die. (We'll learn more about that in the last chapter.)

A prosperous person continues to look for work after he has found a job.

People are funny. If they're out of work, they'll do anything to find a job and even relocate if necessary. They craft a resume designed to impress an employer, highlighting their good work ethics and giving reasons why an employer will be better off hiring them instead of the other fifty applicants.

Once they get the position, it doesn't take long until they start to look for ways to get out of work. Forgetting how difficult it was to obtain the position, they get overconfident. If asked to do something not in their job description, they tell the employer that's not what they're getting paid to do. Now the employer that previously was looking for reasons to hire this person will be looking for reasons to fire him. The employee just gave him one. As an employer myself, when this happens, I keep my eyes open for a replacement.

In the statement above about continuing to look for work after you find a job, I don't mean that when you get hired, you put resume in to other places. What I mean is that when you're given a task and complete it sooner than expected, look for something else to keep busy. If you were an employer, would you look for reasons to get rid of someone with those ethics or look for reasons to keep him? You know what the answer is, so you know the person you need to become.

The Generosity Factor

The Generosity Factor is a book co-written by Ken Blanchard and S. Truett Cathy, founder of Chick-fil-A. He gives credit to God for all his success, and he has built a business with over one thousand locations. When he was asked how many locations he owned, he said, "I don't own any. I manage them for God. He gave them to me to take care of for Him. I give Him 10 percent, and He gives me 90 percent of the profits. I use that 90 percent to help others along the way."

He has honored God through his restaurants by closing on Sunday and putting God first in his business.

S. Truett Cathy has an extravagant business but a modest home. He has given over one thousand six hundred $1,000 scholarships to his employees so they can better their education. He devotes himself to teaching to others what he calls "the generosity factor," which has five principles:

H: He (God) owns all.
E: Every day is an opportunity.
A: Action is required.
R: Remember your blessings.
T: Thank God.
He applies them through the four *t*'s:
Time: Give to God.
Talent: Give to God.
Treasure: Give to God.
Touch: Give to others.
S. Truett Cathy also funds twelve houses for unwanted

children and pays couples full-time wages to run those houses, plus a boys camp and a girls camp to teach them the above formula of the generosity factor.

- *Study, understand, obey* so this transformation can take place.
- *God's laws* are spiritual laws that reach beyond the physical.
- *Generosity* is an attitude that must be cultivated daily.
- Have a *positive influence* on all you come in contact with.

> *"Therefore if anyone is in Christ, he is a new creation: old things have passed away; behold all things have become new" (2 Cor. 5:17).*

Empower others. You cannot help someone to the top of the mountain without getting closer to the summit yourself. A driven person thinks he owns everything. A called person has the attitude that everything is on loan from God. A driven person learns how to make money. A called person learns how to give it away. A driven person achieves great things. A called person serves others and helps them to achieve their goals.

The person who really wants to do something finds a way; others find excuses.

Did you ever ask someone to do something with you or for you or go somewhere with you, and the response was, "That depends on what comes up." Or the person doesn't know what he or she is doing and will let you know. *He or she doesn't want to do it.* Believe me; something will come up that's more important, because to that person, anything else is more important.

If, however, you ask the same question of someone who does want to take you up on your offer, that person will look at his or her calendar to see if he or she has a previous commitment.

If he or she does, that person will change the commitment if possible. Or if that person didn't have anything for that time, he or she will write your cause into his or her calendar. *This person does want to do it.* People will find an excuse not to do what they don't want to do and will find a way to do what they do want to do.

The most difficult part of getting to the top of the ladder of prosperity is getting through the crowd at the bottom.

Many people have a go-nowhere lifestyle. They have a right to choose that lifestyle. If they don't want to move forward in life, they won't. However, many of those people don't want to see anybody get ahead of them. They feel it makes them look bad. They feel it's their responsibility in life to hold others back. If you're going to climb the ladder to the top, you must find your way through that crowd at the bottom. Remember, when you climb a ladder, you take one step at a time. If you attempt to take more, you may stretch yourself too far and get hurt.

Small minds are the first to condemn great ideas.

Don't be too surprised or discouraged when you try to present an idea and someone shoots it down before you can get it out of your mouth. That person is complacent and sees him- or herself as a failure. That person will never look at your idea in a positive way because he or she is so unhappy with his or her own efforts to achieve that he or she doesn't believe anyone else could possibly have a better idea than his or hers, which failed. That person will continue to shoot ideas down. Don't go to this person with an idea. Go to someone who will give an honest appraisal of your idea and look at it positively. You will get a better evaluation to determine if it will work or not. Or you could just move forward with your idea. It is best, however, to move forward with good council.

Many men lie down their lives trying to lay up money.

If laying up money is the purpose for someone's existence,

he or will find him- or herself with a lonely life. There is nothing wrong with saving for a rainy day or something special, but when money becomes the ultimate focus in life, it will destroy the soul. Keep money in proper prospective with the Word of God.

Why We Don't Give

I don't have it to give.

The problem is not that we don't have money to give, it's that we don't have enough faith to give it. Making a choice to consume for oneself instead of giving means that we eat all the seeds God gives us. A seed not planted cannot bring a harvest. What is withheld is divided. We can reap only what we sow.

We should give according to our income, lest God make our income according to our giving. We make all kinds of excuses for not giving. We comfort ourselves in calling them reasons. We attempt to convince God that we can't give any more because of our obligations, when in reality we don't believe or trust God. Can God make our income according to our giving? Will God make our income according to our giving? I believe so. Perhaps not in the amount we get per week, but if we withhold from God, our money will not go nearly as far or accomplish what we intend it to accomplish. So when you give, give in a way that when God makes your income according to your giving, it will be a raise.

I'm barely making ends meet now. I can't afford to give.

When you're barely making ends meet, you can't afford *not* to give. How can you have this attitude and ask God to deliver you out of debt? How can you possibly have enough faith for God to deliver you when you ask with an unbelieving spirit? An unbelieving spirit doubts God's Word. God cannot answer a prayer that is conceived in doubt in a positive way. Doubt is caused by fear, the opposite of faith.

- Doubt and fear say, "If I give, I'll lose."
- Faith says, "If I give, I cannot lose. I'll always win."

Can we pray for God to deliver us from debt, knowing that by refusing to tithe, our finances are under the curse? But what about our giving after we tithe? Remember the words of Jesus: *"Inasmuch as ye have done it unto one of the least of these my brethren, ye have done it unto me"* (Matt. 25:40). When we give to those in need for God's cause, we're giving to Jesus. When we say no, we are really saying no to Jesus.

By withholding our giving, we rob ourselves of many blessings of future harvests that come from the concept of giving and receiving. If we don't have the faith that God will honor His promise in giving back pressed down and running over, how can we have the faith that He'll deliver us from our debt? If we lack action and do not give when we see a need, what we hold back will not be blessed. Only what we release and give will be blessed. *Giving will grow our income; withholding will grow our debt.* Fear and doubt cause us to think if we give to God, we'll lose and not have for ourselves. God's Word teaches that to give is gain and to withhold is loss.

We attempt to circumvent God's Word and make God play by our rules (which would make God our servant rather than being His servant). It may be that we are barely making ends meet because we do not believe in God's Word enough to trust Him.

If I give any more, I'll lose my house, car, and furniture.

This is a tough position to be in and one that's a test of faith. I've been there and had to make that decision. I have found God faithful. He does deliver on His promise. God tells us that He will give back pressed down and running over.

- We must believe God.
- We must trust God.
- We must make the following decision: am I going to put my car, home, and electric before God and then expect God to bless me financially?
- We must come to the point to be willing to give up these things and take God at His Word.

Clarification—the tithe is a must, giving an option. If we hold back the tithe or part of it, the part we hold back is under God's curse and the part we give is under God's blessing. The curse is not mentioned under gifts and offerings. Therefore our finances are not under a curse if we withhold giving; however, what we give will be under God's blessings and be returned, pressed down, shaken together, and run over unto our feet. They are opportunities to fulfill the heart of giving.

Putting God first means putting Him before—not after—our homes, cars, utilities, and so on. What we place before God falls out from under His blessing. Did you ever place those things before God and have your car break down? You ask God for help to get it fixed and find your prayer unanswered. Think about it. You withhold from God because you don't believe or trust Him, yet you expect Him to put your prayers on top of His priority list. God answers the prayers of the believer, not the doubter. Where is God on your priority list?

The further down on the list we place God on our list of priorities, the less significant He becomes. The higher we place Him on the list, the more significant He becomes. The more significant He becomes, the more we see Him actively working in our lives.

If you do make the decision to give to God first, you may lose your car, home, or electric. When you put God first, knowing He will not be indebted to you, He'll give you a better car, house, or whatever. We can never give anything up for God's purpose that He does not give us much better than we had.

Placing God first when we're in dire need brings the greatest blessings. Not placing Him first brings us greater needs. The greatest test of our faith is giving when we ourselves are in great need. It is at these times that we see the miraculous powers of God's Word coming to life, when God brings us the greatest blessings. In chapter 11 we'll address the widow's mite. She gave all she had. Make sure you read this fantastic witness of faith.

I'm giving everything I can now.

No, you're giving everything you have the *faith* to give now. You can't lose by giving, only by withholding.

<u>Stretching Our Faith</u>

Stretch your giving and then stretch some more. When you stretch your giving, you're stretching your faith. For example, if you take a rubber band and stretch it, the more you stretch, it the weaker it gets. If you stretch it far enough, it will break. Remember that God's laws are just the opposite of natural laws. When you trust God and stretch your faith, stretch it some more and then more. The more you stretch it, the stronger it gets. No matter how far you stretch faith, you can never ever break it.

I'm not making enough to give a dime.

If you're making a dollar, you can give a dime. If you're making more than that, this statement comes from lack of belief and not a lack of money.

The church is always asking for money, money, money. Enough is enough.

God's work depends upon God's people giving in faith. It is not mandatory; it is optional. However, you may be looking at this the wrong way. Turn it around. The need for funds indicates that someone is going to receive the news of the gospel—someone who may not have heard it otherwise. This is yet another opportunity for God to bless you.

If you treat giving as a curse, it will be a curse to you. If you treat giving as a blessing, it will be a blessing to you. The choice is in your hands. Do you want your finances to be a curse or a blessing in your life? The more you give, the more blessed you are.

Giving has nothing to do with the amount of money or possessions we have. It's an attitude of gratitude. If we are grateful, we will give if we are not grateful, we will not give.

It is interesting the responses you get when you ask people to give for a cause. They are all over the gamut; many are negative. When you reach for someone's wallet, he or she resents it. When you touch his or her heart, he or she reaches for his or her own wallet.

A pastor once asked a businessman to give to a cause. "You Christians!" the businessman said. "All you want to do is give, give, give."

The pastor hesitated and then answered, "Thank you."

"For what?" the businessman said. "I haven't given you anything."

"Thank you," the pastor said, "for the best definition of a Christian that I have ever heard."

Another response is, "I give to so many causes now. Every time I open my mail, there is someone with a worthy cause that just has to have more money." It is unfortunate, but many of these mail order giving programs are scams. Many funds are used for self–improvement and not ministry improvement. Before giving, make sure the money is used for what it's being solicited for and for a worthy cause. Pray and investigate. If it's a good cause, you can't go wrong by giving; however, it is prudent to choose the cause you wish to be a part of and concentrate in that area of ministry.

Here's a good test to see if the ministry is a good cause: anyone who solicits you to give for selfish reasons is going to use your money for selfish gain. In other words, if they tell you to give so you can get a new car, boat, or house, they're actually telling you what they're going to do with your money after they get it. They're going to buy a new car, boat, or house. There is no place in the Bible that instructs us to give for our own selfish desires. We are to give out of love for God and others. We are to give because there is a need in ministry in harvesting of souls. We are to give because the Lord asks us to.

I shouldn't give with expectation of receiving.

This sounds noble; however, it's used by many as an excuse not to give. It's not right to give for selfish gain and use it as a moneymaking scheme, to give for the purpose of just making money and expecting a large return. There is no place in the Bible that instructs us to give for our own selfish desires. We are to give out of love of God and others. We are to give because there is a need in ministry in harvesting of souls. We are to give because the Lord asks us to. Our benefit from giving is a natural result of God fulfilling His promise to us.

I've heard TV evangelists telling the audience to give to their ministry and God will give them a new Cadillac, a new home, or a new boat. When you hear this, turn the other way. When they solicit your giving for selfish gain, they will use it for selfish gain.

It is, however, proper to give to God's ministry and expect a return, if it is given in faith. If you don't expect a return, you don't expect God to keep His Word. Would you pray and not expect an answer? Would you take up an offering in a church and not expect to get anything in the plate? Would you work for a week and not expect a paycheck? Give as the purpose in your own heart but expect and look for blessings to come. If you don't expect God to deliver on His Word, you will be reluctant to give to another cause.

If I give any more, I'll be in the poorhouse.

I can accept this if anyone could show me one person in two thousand years who ended up in the poorhouse because he gave too much to God. There are many, however, who are in the poorhouse because they misused, abused, and squandered the funds with which God blessed them.

I can't give any more and put food on the table.

One of the basic promises of God is to feed you, clothe you, and give you shelter. If you have the attitude that it's you who puts the food on your table, you are removing God from the equation and that area of your life cannot be blessed by God.

Generosity has nothing to do with wealth. Most stingy people use poverty as an excuse not to be generous. A generous person will find a way to be generous. A stingy person will find a way to be stingy. Are these true reasons for not giving, excuses, lies, or just a plain lack of faith? Whatever the cause, make sure you're being truthful to God because He knows the real reason. It is because of your generosity or lack of it.

Believe

The belief always comes before the harvest. The sowing always comes because of the belief. The harvest comes as a result of the sowing the seed. A seed not sown is a seed not grown.

We must have Christ revealed to us if we are ever going to reveal Him to others. When Christ is revealed to us, we will not have a problem with the concept of sowing and reaping.

- When we know Christ, we believe Him.
- When we believe Christ, we trust Him.
- When we trust Christ, we give.

Christ isn't valued at all unless He is valued above all. Can Christ be valued above all but your money? No. The way we express that belief is through our giving.

Seek God first, and the things you want will seek you. God knows our wants and needs before we ask for them. If we seek God first and sow, the things we want will come looking for us.

Nothing worth having is secured by sin. Nothing worth keeping is lost in serving God. Don't ever be drawn away by the supposed success of those who obtained their wealth illegally through deceitful means. Believe me, you don't want to be in their shoes. If you are going to secure anything, be honest, sincere, and trustworthy.

A person is never what he or she ought to be until he or she is doing what he or she ought to be doing. A person ought to be doing the will of God.

Give 100 percent effort where you are. God will move you where you ought to be. You may be saying, "There is so much to do. Where do I start?" The answer is start where you are right now. Pray for God to guide and direct you to a need. He will.

If God can get it through you, God will give it to you. God never lies. God never fails. His promises are always greater than our needs. There is no need on this earth that any human can have that cannot be covered by God's promises. Who are the recipients of these promises? Those who have believed in Jesus and accepted Him as Lord and Savior of their souls and those who walk by faith.

Do not forget that God is between you and your enemy. Anyone coming against God's children is coming against God. God will repay them tenfold—for good or evil. Someone who harms a child of God has God to answer to. Believe me, you do not have to even think of getting back or even with them. Instead, pray for them, leave them in God's hands, and move forward, because His judgment is sure and just. It may seem like it is not going to happen, but rest assured it will come.

The church that is not a missionary church will soon be a mission church. Every church is perceived by the community as either being a missionary church or a mission church. You've heard it said that a heart without Jesus is a mission field and a heart with Jesus is a missionary.

If a church is consistently going into the community to get

people to support the church or its cause, asking the community to help pay for a church need or project, in the eyes of the community, that church is a mission church. The community ministers to the need of the church. The community thinks, *That church cannot survive without us. They need us. Without us that church would have to close its doors.*

On the other hand, if a church is consistently going into the community to meet the needs of the people, helping, feeding, witnessing, praying, offering friendship and understanding in their hour of need, this church is looked upon as a missionary church that ministers to the community. In the people's eyes, the community could not survive without that church. They need the church. They think, *What would our community do without that church?*

Which kind of church did Christ call His church to be? What kind of church is your church?

So it is with every individual. We are either a mission field or a missionary. Into which category do you fall?

My late uncle, Jack Butler, and his wife, Mary, were missionaries most of their adult lives. They were affiliated with the New Tribes Mission headquartered in Sanford, Florida. Uncle Jack took me to the headquarters to meet some of the missionaries who worked there. I say missionaries because that is what they are. They work an eight-hour day, but none are paid. They depend upon their missionary support, and they never ask for it; they pray for it. He introduced me to the director. As I shook his hand, he asked me a strange question: "When did God call you into missions?" This caught me off guard. I didn't believe I was called to be a missionary. Grabbing for an answer, I explained that I taught youth Sunday school at my church in Greenville, Pennsylvania. He asked me again, "When did God call you to the mission field?" Still struggling for an answer, I told him that I was on the board of trustees at my church. He asked me again, "When did God call you to the mission field?" I told him that

I work with the Gideons and distribute Bibles. Guess what? He asked me again, "When did God call you to the mission field?" I then realized that he was asking me when I received Jesus into my heart as Lord. That was the day I, as well as every other Christian, became a missionary. Are you a missionary?

Giving

For as long as we live, we must give. That is one of the joys of living. Perhaps some of us have wished that the time might come when we need not give anymore. Then we need to read this true little message in verse:

For giving is living, the angel said.
God feeds to the hungry sweet charity's bread.
And must I keep giving again and again?
My selfish and querulous answer ran.
Oh, no! said the angel, piercing me through.
Just give till God stops giving to you. (*Sunday School Times*)

Giving is not an obligation. It is an opportunity an opportunity to place ourselves between God and a need to be filled. We allow God to flow through us and to the need. In doing so, God blesses the person or place given to, the cause, and the person doing the giving. It's more blessed to give than to receive. Remember, God does not multiply what we have. He can multiply only what we give. What we have is God's gift to us. What we give is our gift to God.

Chapter 9 Action Project

I will do the following:

1. Stretch my giving by 10 percent for thirty days.
2. Then stretch it again.

3. Remember that I don't give because I have; I have because I give.
4. Give out of my need and know that God will not be indebted to me in my area of need.
5. Give because God instructs me to do so.
6. Give because I love God.
7. Give because it is more blessed to give than to receive.

Chapter 10: Sowing and Reaping

DISSATISFACTION and discouragement are not caused by the absence of things but the absence of vision.

> *"Where there is no revelation, the people cast off restraint"* *(Prov.29:18a).*

Have you ever run into someone who can't tell you where they came from, where they are, where they're going, or what they're going to do when they get there? They are those with unhappy, unfruitful lives, just hopping from one flower to the other and going whichever way the wind is blowing. They don't have any control over their surroundings, so they become victims of their surroundings. Other people's thoughts, ideas, and plans form their futures. They live meaningless lives and die unhappy.

This is why God encourages us to form a vision, not from

our own mind but from His. Our visions for the future are usually selfish and self-serving. God's vision is unselfish and God-serving. If we sincerely pray for God to send us vision, He will. Just be patient. Happiness comes in the journey of fulfilling the vision, not necessarily at the end when we attain it. On that journey we need to understand the following concepts.

We Cannot Outgive God

> *"But seek first the kingdom of God, and His righteousness; and all these things shall be added unto you" (Matt. 6:33).*

When we seek the Kingdom first with our seed, we need not fear being wiped out. We work so hard at getting things added to us and never achieve peace in the process. Only when we seek God first and His righteousness will we be in a position to receive. We are in a microwave society. We want it, and we want it now. The Word tells us to seek God first and *all* of these things *will* be added unto us.

God's people are managers of God's Kingdom. God will help us do what we're willing to do for ourselves. God gives us all the tools of His Kingdom, gives us directions on how to manage it, but we need to do it. We find ourselves praying and expecting God to do all the work. Wow, wouldn't that be the life of Riley? God doesn't want us lazy; He wants us faithful.

The farmer who sows does not lose his seed; he gains a crop. It seems that no matter what God says, we seem to somehow hang onto our worldly thinking of if we give, we're going to lose. It can't happen. There are two types of givers: people who give what's left over and people who live on what's left over. We all fall into one of these categories (or perhaps you've created one in between). I'm sure you've already answered which one you're in. If you're in the first category, you're giving Christ the crumbs that fall off your table. You're the only one who determines if you move to the second category and live on what's left over.

When viewing wealth from God's perspective, you'll see the thing to fear isn't giving too much but sowing too little. Even though the majority of Christians fear giving too much, they can also testify that the losses they experience are not from giving to God or others but in keeping too much for themselves.

If you keep what you have, that is your reward. Your reward contains a multitude of seeds. What you release is your seed. When you release your seed, you're trading a small present seed for a large future harvest. Remember, the seed already contains the fruit. It just needs to be planted so more fruit can grow.

Techniques and methods change, but principles never do. The principles God laid down in His Word never change. Man has tried and tried to change them but has been unsuccessful every time. Yet we still continue to try. If we could use that energy in believing and doing God's Word God's way, we would evangelize the whole world in less than ten years. Stick with God's principles, and you can never go wrong.

> *"But this I say, he who sows sparingly will also reap sparingly; and he who sows bountifully will also reap bountifully"* *(2 Cor. 9:6).*

This is a law that God lays down and the law that cannot be broken: Sow sparingly, reap sparingly. Sow bountifully, reap bountifully. God has placed the decision of our prosperity in our hands. *How much we have is directly related to what we give.*

Why is it that when things go right, we want to take all the credit, and when things go wrong, we want to blame someone or something anyone but ourselves? When something goes wrong, it's good to get into the habit of looking at ourselves first for an outside possibility that we may be part of or the entire problem. Our problems will get solved more quickly.

> *"Knowing that whatsoever good anyone does, he will receive the same from the Lord, whether he is slave or free" (Eph. 6:8).*

- We *know* no guesswork.
- The good we do is *always* rewarded by God.
- It makes no difference if we are subject to someone else who has authority over us.

No one can stop God from bringing us rewards. We worry so much about our enemies or competitors trying to stop us from getting ahead that we lose sight of the fact that they cannot—repeat, *cannot*—stop our God from blessing us. Those who try to stop the work God has given us to do will only find that the more they attempt to stop us, God blesses us that much more.

It is God who does the rewarding, even if man doesn't recognize your deeds. If you're an employer who risks it all or an employee with a dead-end job, it is God who brings the blessing. He will bless you where you are or move you to where you need to be for that blessing to come to pass. Don't ever feel that God cannot bless you where you are. That is doubt. Wherever you are, whatever you're doing, God can still find a way to bless you. It could be that you're so absorbed in what's being done to you that you can't see the blessings God has for you.

God has hidden a multitude of blessings in the hardships we encounter.

My wife, Laverne, and I were at a peanut festival in New Bethlehem, Pennsylvania, when I noticed several chestnut trees. It had been a long time since I'd seen one. When I was young, I used to pick them. They were plentiful until blight killed them. That's why I was so surprised to see them. Laverne, who was unfamiliar with them, touched one and got pricked by one of the many needles covering the shell that protected the nut inside. The needles are encased in a semi-hard crust. Removing the crust reveals a brown leatherlike shell. Roast that shell in a fire, and it can be removed to get to a very tasty nut. Nothing tastes better than a warm chestnut.

God has food for us in all situations in life, some of which are unpleasant and at times harmful. These trying circumstances can bring disappointment, which leads to discouragement. We admit defeat and stop trying. We're enslaved to the problem we can't seem to be able to solve. We realize we can't achieve success by our own power and need a higher power to succeed. It's at that point that we decide either to trust God or be convinced that even God cannot help. If we trust God when we're at our wits' end and take the next step toward solving the problem, in that step is where we meet God. Our faith in Him brings us the rest of the way. We just have to place one foot after the other in the direction of the blessing we know we can't have without God's help. These are also the times we decide that, with God's help, all things are possible through Jesus Christ our Lord.

If we stop where our physical capabilities end, we'd never see the blessings protected by the needles, coating, and hard shell. We need to train our spiritual eyes to see problems or obstacles in life as protection for God's blessings that are inside. But to get to the nugget of blessing, we must remove that protective covering not by our own power or might but by the power of God.

If we stop where our physical capabilities end, we'll never go any further in the journey of life than where we are at this moment.

Sowing for Selfish Reasons

> *"Be not deceived; God is not mocked: for whatsoever*
> *a man sow, that will he also reap. For he who sows to*
> *his flesh will of the flesh reap corruption. but he that*
> *sows to the Spirit will of the Spirit reap everlasting life"*
> *(Gal. 6:7–8).*

If we use God's Word as a moneymaking tool for ourselves and give so that we can have luxury items, it is mocking God. If we mock God, He promises that we will reap corruption. God has given us power to make those decisions.

Our actions, the way we do business, the way we treat others always, always, always comes back to us. We know that sharing with others from that which we need for ourselves will all come back to us, sometimes tenfold and sometimes a hundredfold. This includes love, lending a helping hand, and words of encouragement, as well as giving of our finances.

We sow the seed in God's garden, not our own. When we sow in God's garden, He gives us plenty of fruit for our own that is our reward. Seeds in God's garden find good soil. If we sow in sinful soil, we reap sinful results and multiply the bad things that come our way. There is enough bad in this world without multiplying it. Sowing in God's garden multiplies the good in our lives. Believe me, we would be much easier for others to get along with by sowing in God's good soil.

What We Plant, We Reap

> *"But God has chosen the foolish things of the world to*
> *put to shame the wise; and God has chosen the weak*
> *things of the world to put to shame the things which are*
> *mighty" (1 Cor. 1:27).*

When we prosper using God's principles, the world cannot understand it because God's principles are completely opposite of the way worldly success is achieved. The world is so confounded that it can't believe it. Please don't think for a moment that you're going to impress the world and the ungodly by prospering God's way. They will see it, but they will never believe it. They will only believe it when they too find Jesus. We need to point them toward Jesus and not to our successes. Let our successes speak for themselves.

The only things impossible to us are the things we limit by our own lack of faith, thus limiting God. The word *impossible* is found only in the dictionary of fools. That isn't a new phrase; it's been around for a long time. The reason it's been around for so long is that it has been a proven fact in every conceivable situation.

> *"And He said the kingdom of God, as if a man should scatter seed on the ground; and should sleep by night , and rise by day, and the seed should sprout and grow, he himself does not know how" (Mark 4:26–27).*

God brings from areas that we don't expect and ways that are of His doing and not our own. Narrow is the path to righteousness, but broad is the way to destruction. Confidence comes from our physical and mental abilities; *"faith comes from hearing and hearing from the word of God"* (Rom. 10:17). It originates not with our minds but with God's will. God's will is believed by the mind before we will begin to act. When we act and apply God's spiritual application to our physical, we rest the outcome in the hand of God.

With worldly thinking, we attempt to get our spiritual belief to follow our physical needs. These are the chains that need to be broken if we are to follow God His way. God wants us to be led by the Spirit and to have the physical follow the Spirit rather than be led by the physical and attempt to force the Spirit to follow us. Remember the story of the pilot and the copilot. God doesn't want to be our copilot to go with us where we want to take Him and help when we break down. He wants to be the pilot to take us where He wants us to go and for us to help Him in His work.

Experience is the best teacher of all. There are many good teachers out there, but it's not until you put knowledge into practice that you really learn. God uses the phrase of putting us through the trials of fire in order to get rid of the impurities within our spiritual lives.

> *"As you have done, it shall be done unto you: your reprisal shall return unto your own head"* (Obad. 1:15).

Do you believe it? The rewards that we receive are directly related to the seeds we sow. What we do to or for others will come back upon our own heads. Man may never see the good we do, but God always does.

Caution: We need to choose our words carefully when dealing with positive or negative situations in our lives. The words we speak are seeds of a different sort but seeds just the same. When we speak, we are planting a seed in someone's ear. It is true that some of those seeds will fall by the wayside to be of no effect and choked out. Many of our words, however, will find root and move to the heart, where they will be watered, and move on to the soul, where they come to fruitage. Without our realizing it, our words can make a change in the lives of others for the positive or negative. Through the seed of our words, we have the power to

- make someone feel good or bad about themselves;
- give encouragement or discouragement;
- help them become successful or failure; or
- lead them to Christ or drive them away.

Be careful what you say, because in due season every word we speak will come back on our own heads for good or bad, just like the words others speak to you come back upon them.

My suggestion to you is choose your words carefully in every situation. We never know who they will affect.

> *"The Lord your God will make you abound in all the work of your hand, in the fruit of your body, in the increase of your livestock, and in the produce of your land for good" (Deut. 30:9).*

All that we put a hand to, God will make plenteous. Trying times are no time to quit trying. When you're in the middle of a trial, problem, or hardship, you need to try harder and not give up. At the end is our reward. God brings us through trials so He may equip us to be in a position to help others. He puts before us someone going through the same trial. Had we not gone through it ourselves, we wouldn't understand what others are going through or what they need to get through it themselves. That person may very well be the reason God let you go through the trial. Some trials are brought by God, some He allows, but His promise is that if we keep the faith, He will bring us through them all.

You may be in business and have great ambition of success. You want to achieve and do well. However, it seems that there are many obstacles that need to be overcome. It seems like the harder you attempt to overcome them, the more resistance you encounter. You get weary and run-down and just feel like quitting. What do you do?

Remember, the obstacles may be the reason you have been chosen for the job to begin with. For example, if pipes didn't break, there would be no need for a plumber. If house roofs didn't wear, there would be no need for roofers. Obstacles are good. They provide job security. The more pipes break, the more the plumber makes.

Sit back and take a look at your own occupation. Perceive obstacles as opportunities and don't be tempted to take the easy path. Rewards for the easy path are few, but removing obstacles is highly rewarded. What about life situations we find ourselves in—hardships that come our way, such as accidents, illnesses, or deaths of loved ones? Unfortunately, these are events that come to every one of us sooner or later. How we handle them depends upon how we have seen others handle them. We're taught by someone else who has gone through the same situation and come out the other end successfully.

This could also cause us the most problems. If the others we're following were wrong, so are we. This causes us to continually make the same mistakes over and over without knowing why. Unless we find another way, we'll never have an answer to our own difficulties. It's like the blind leading the blind.

This is why we need to turn to God. God never fails, always loves, and is always right. There is no other being in the world that can say that. We need to be open to hear, read, and do what God asks us to do, the way He wants it done. Then we'll be in a position to help others going through the same set of problems. Only such sight can lead the blind confidently to restore their own sight so they can see the end of the difficulty. They too will be in a position to help others.

> *"Strive to enter through the narrow gate: for many, I say to you, will seek to enter, and will not be able"* *(Luke 13:24).*

> *"I press toward the goal for the prize of the upward call of God in Christ Jesus" (Phil. 3:14).*

Remember, it gets darkest just before the break of dawn. Don't ever give up. Set your sights on the vision the Lord has given you to follow and don't let obstacles stop you. Just when you feel like giving up may be the time the obstacle is ready to break down. If you give up, the obstacle or problem wins and regains strength.

Our Ceilings

A ceiling in a house determines how much space you have to live in. The lower the ceiling, the smaller the space. Some ceilings, like those in attics, are so low you have to bend over to walk. This restricts your movement and ability to function. You can even develop disabilities walking stooped over all the time. Who would want to live in an attic? There are some rooms with low ceilings that people live in by choice. The only way to get more room is to move to a larger room or raise the ceiling.

What does that have to do with our topic? In the journey of life, we all develop ceilings—the space we decide to live in, a place of comfort. These are limits we set for ourselves that determine how far we can go in life or what we can achieve through our vocations or Christian walks. We learn to live within the boundaries of these ceilings. The sad thing is that the majority of Christians entrap themselves by living in attics when God has prepared mansions for them. They live far beneath the blessings God has for them. Because of their self-made ceilings, their movement is restricted, and they go through life suffering needlessly. They don't have the funds to move to another larger room and don't have the education or willingness to raise the ceiling. So it is in life. Raising the ceiling is a choice, not a mandate. We can make life a prison by refusing to raise the ceiling.

How do you raise the ceiling? Remember the following thoughts, and you'll never look at a problem or obstacle the same way again:

- The more persistent you are in moving against a problem or obstacle, the weaker the obstacle gets. Keep going, and eventually that weakness will give in to your persistence and you will overcome. Keep the faith, and the reward of overcoming is yours.

Your own power may not be enough, but remember that *with God all things are possible.*

- If you give up, the problem, obstacle, or situation is strengthened and gains power in your life. It will wear and tear you down and eventually destroy you.

Overcoming trying times is not situational but decisional. The Lord never told us we would not have trying times. He does give us assurance that He will see us through to the end.

On Humility and Giving

"Trust in the LORD and do good; Dwell in the land, and feed on His faithfulness"(Ps. 37:3).

"He that gives to the poor will not lack: but he who hides his eyes will have many curses. When the wicked arise, men hide themselves: but when they perish, the righteous increase" (Prov. 28:27–28).

"For whoever exalts himself will be humbled, and he who humbles himself will be exalted" (Luke 14:11).

Humility is just denying self and doing God's will. When we lift ourselves up, God will bring us down. When we submit to God's will and not think too highly of ourselves, God will lift us up. Many of us have a strange view of humility. Some feel that they are being humble if they have a talent and have to be begged to use it or if they have money and pretend to be poor. That is not humility but bordering on stupidity. If you have a talent, God wants you to use it for Him. If you have money, God wants you to use it for His work. Please do not get stewardship confused with humility.

If a restaurant gives good service, it results in repeat business.

The same applies to good stewards. God wants to give to you so you can give to His work. And if you sow generously, God is able to give you more and more. Replace the word *I* in your conversations with *He*. Give credit where credit is due. Sometimes I find myself saying the word *I* when I should be saying *He*. God is the life and the light of man. Being that God is life, if you remove God from this world, all would die. Nothing could live without the Giver of Life. There is nothing we can do or achieve that we should not give God the credit for.

> *"His Lord said to him, well done, good and faithful servant; you have been faithful over few things, I will make you ruler over many things: enter into the joy of thy Lord" (Mat. 25:23).*

Whatever God gives you to do, do the best you can, and God will exalt you no matter what you're doing. Even if you're doing something you don't like, do it to the best of your ability. Even if no man can see you doing it, God can. He is ever present. So don't ever think that your good deeds go unnoticed. This includes in the workplace. No matter where you are or what you're doing, nothing and nobody can stop God from blessing you. God brings Christians into deep water not to drown them but to cleanse them. When confronted with difficulties, don't ask, "Why is God doing this to me?" Instead ask, "Why is God allowing me to go through this?" It is then that you can see blessings in disguise.

> *"God resist the proud, gives grace to the humble" (1 Pet. 5:5b).*

> *"It is more blessed to give than to receive" (Acts 20:35b).*

It's a natural human response to place more emphasis on

getting than giving. But what's natural to humans is unnatural to God. What's natural to us is striving to get for ourselves or waiting for someone to do it for us. After all, we've been doing that since we were infants. Sitting back and getting requires no effort. On the other hand, we can work every day to get more. But we find the more we get, the less happy we are.

Whatever comes naturally to us, think the opposite. We need to change our mindsets from getting to giving. Since giving doesn't come natural to most, we must be aware of it at all times. This requires effort. Don't think, *What can I get?* but *Where can I give?* That thinking will bring blessings you won't have room to receive.

When we give little, it hurts. This may sound like a strange statement, but it's true just the same. We have to look at the reason we give little to begin with. One could say it's because we have little, but most of the time that's an excuse instead of a reason. We give little because we doubt God and fear loss. Otherwise, there would be no problem parting with something we need ourselves for the benefit of one who has a greater need. You see, God does not bless us through a channel of fear; he blesses us through the channel of faith. *"According to our faith, let it be done unto us"* (Mat. 9:29).

When we give abundantly, it feels good. Statistics prove that people who give abundantly are much happier than those who don't. The Lord tells us that it's more blessed to give than to receive. Think about the last time you gave to a good cause. It made you feel good, didn't it? That feeling lasts and doesn't fade. Now think about the last time you received. How did you feel? Some feel embarrassed, some feel ashamed, others graciously accept another person's kindness. Incidentally, we shouldn't be too proud to accept the gift.

Getting is proportional to giving:

- Give by the teaspoon, receive by the teaspoon.
- Give by the tablespoon, receive by the tablespoon.

• Give by the barrel, receive by the barrel.

God will, by your faith, inspire others to give unto you. To train others to do the same, you must tell and demonstrate, lead and not push. You'll get more followers by setting the example than telling them how to do something. Remember, many Christians have not broken away from worldly thinking yet. They may have to see to believe. Once they see, it sets the example and they do. Only then can they too receive blessings. Blessings cannot be received by what someone else does. We can see them and be blessed by seeing them but cannot experience for ourselves until we do. Doing inspires others.

You can't walk backward into the future. Everybody knows this is impossible. Yet why do people keep trying? Many Christians are hanging onto past failures and use them as excuses for not achieving in the present, thus destroying their own futures. We have the past to learn from, not live in. If you let the past control your present, you will have no future. You will go no further than you are right now.

If you're not happy with where you are in life, it's up to you to change where you are. You can't change your lot in life by standing still. You need to envision what you want out of life and move in that direction, knowing without doubt that you have a God who will help you get there. You have to take the first step in faith before you can expect God to step in and help. It may be impossible for you, but it's not for God. You need to make the decision or else nothing changes. God wants to help you move forward, but you have to want to be helped.

What is given away cannot be taken away. When you give something away, you don't ever have to worry about someone stealing it from you. It can't be done. So, if you're worrying day and night that someone will steal something from you, give it away. Thieves will never find it at your place.

"Let him who stole, steal no longer, but rather let him

labor, working with his hands what is good, that he may have something to give him who has need" (Eph. 4:28).

The reason God blesses us is so that we will have to give to those who need.

"So let each one give as he purposes in his heart, not grudgingly or of necessity; for God loves a cheerful giver" (2 Cor. 9:7).

If you give out of fear, necessity, or a sense of duty, you resent it. Great trials are often necessary to prepare us for great responsibilities. Trials are a reality in everyone's life. We don't like them, and we don't ask for them. If we had the choice, we would never go through them. Yet by avoiding them, we deprive ourselves of great responsibilities.

A Christian, But ...

Pardon me, Honorable Judge, you see, I am a Christian; I am a new man in Christ. It was not my new man but the old man that did the wrong," said the self-excusing culprit on trial. To this the judge is reported to have replied, "Since it was the old man that did the wrong, we'll sentence him to thirty days in jail. And inasmuch as the new man had complicity with the old man in the wrong, we'll give him thirty days also. You will therefore go to jail for sixty days.
—*Gospel Herald*

The Dog Learned Quickly

An old lady rented furnished villas for the summer, and with the villa a large dog was included. In the sitting room of the villa there was a very comfortable arm chair. The old lady liked this chair better than any other in the house. She always made for it the first thing. But alas! She nearly always found the chair occupied by the large dog. Being afraid of the dog, she never dared hit it to get out of the chair, but instead she would go to the window and call, "Cats!" The dog would rush to the window and bark, and the old lady would quietly slip into the vacated chair.

One day the dog entered the room and found the old lady in possession of the chair. He strolled over to the window and, looking out, appeared very much excited, and set up a tremendous barking. The old lady rose and hastened to the window to see what was the matter, and the dog quietly climbed into the chair which suggest that the deceits we practice on others will, sooner or later, be repaid against ourselves. (*Religious Telescope*)

10 Things God Won't Ask You

1. God won't ask what kind of car you drive. He'll ask how many people you drove who didn't have transportation.
2. God won't ask the square footage of your house. He'll ask how many people you welcomed into your home.
3. God won't ask about the clothes you had in your closet. He'll ask how many you helped to clothe.
4. God won't ask what your highest salary was. He'll ask if you compromised your character to obtain it.
5. God won't ask what your job title was. He'll ask if you performed your job to the best of your ability.
6. God won't ask how many friends you had. He'll ask how many people to whom you were a friend.
7. God won't ask in what neighborhood you lived. He'll ask how you treated your neighbors.

8. God won't ask about the color of your skin. He'll ask about the content of your character.
9. God won't ask how much you made your business grow. He'll ask how much you helped others to grow.
10. God won't ask if you loved and worshipped Him. He'll ask how much you loved and worshipped your parents, how much you loved and worshipped your gods on earth.

—Author Unknown

Chapter 10 Action Project

I will do the following:

1. Recognize that I am the one who decides the degree of my prosperity.
2. Recognize that I cannot refuse to plant seeds and expect God to bless the crop.
3. Recognize that I will reap to the degree in which I sow.
4. Refuse to resent giving and look for people's needs toward which I have the opportunity to give.

Chapter 11: Biblical Value of Our Gifts

Our Values vs. God's Values

Before we can completely understand the biblical concept of giving and receiving, we need to have an understanding of the biblical value of our gifts. Our values are different than God's values.

Our Values Constantly Change

We value gifts according to the physical nature of the gift and what it means to us. God values gifts according to the spiritual nature of the gift and what it means to Him. How we determine values are in relation to the monetary value of an item. We value money according to its purchasing power.

Our values constantly change depending on what we purchase and from whom we purchase it. You go into a store downtown, make a purchase, and pay a certain price. You walk across the street and find the same item for far less money. What changed crossing the street? Is the value of our money less in one store than another?

In some countries our currency is worth more than in

others. What changes? The value of the currency. Another country doesn't have the same value for our currency as we do. So it is from state to state, climate to climate, store to store, gas station to gas station, market competition, taxes, bank interest rates—all have an effect on the value of our money. In some places it won't go as far as in others.

If we're basing our futures on a monetary system that is constantly changing, we're walking on a very slippery slope. Depending on an unstable system could leave us empty. Is there no answer? Is there anything we can depend on for sure? Is there something we can know without a doubt will never let us down? The answer is a resounding *yes*!

God's Values Never Change

God is not dependent on our worldly monetary system to bless His children or fulfill His promises. The world system, however, depends upon God. Could the reason there is so much turmoil in the world today be that governments have turned away from God? Any country that is faithful and serving God will be under the blessing and prosperity of God. On the other hand, any country that turns away from God, God will turn away from it, and it will be under God's curse.

A Little Girl's Pennies

God tells us in the Scriptures that "all the earth and the fullness thereof" are His, including the beasts of the field, the fowls of the air, all the silver and gold, and every human soul (Ps. 24:1; Ps. 50:11; Hag. 2:8; Ezek. 18:4). Where did this all come from? God spoke it into existence in just six days. Can He not speak prosperity into our lives? God can grow the biggest trees from our smallest seeds of faith. Nothing illustrates this more than a story published in the *Christian Herald* titled, "A Little Girl's Pennies":

Tattie Wiatt, a little girl, came to a small Sunday school and asked to be taken in, but it was explained there was no room for her. In less than two years she fell ill and slipped away on her own little last pilgrimage, and no one guessed her strange little secret until beneath her pillow was found a torn pocketbook with fifty-seven pennies in it, wrapped in a scrap of paper on which was written, "To help build the little Temple bigger, so that more children can go to Sunday school."

For two years she had saved her pennies for the cause which was nearest her heart. The pastor told the incident to his congregation, and the people began making donations for the enlargement. The papers told it far and wide, and within five years those fifty-seven pennies had grown to be $250,000. Today in Philadelphia can be seen a great church, the Baptist Temple, seating 3,300, Temple College with accommodations for more than 1,400 students, Temple Hospital, and a Temple Sunday school so large that all who wish may come and be comfortable. She was only a little girl, but who can estimate the result of her unselfishness, and her fifty-seven pennies? (*The Christian Herald*)

Is the value of her gift the value of what fifty-seven cents would purchase? No. Fifty-seven cents will not buy us a cup of coffee today. Is it the value of the $250,000, the initial sum raised as result of her gift? No. Is the value the sum of all buildings built as result? No.

All the values above are constantly changing. At the time of Tattie Wiatt's untimely death, you could have bought a cup of coffee for ten cents. Today is would be $1.35. To get a proper description of the value of our gift, we go to one of the most touching stories in the Bible: the account of the widow's mite.

The Widow's Mite

Now Jesus sat opposite the treasury and saw how the

> *people put money into the treasury. And many who were rich put in much. Then one poor widow came and put in two mites, which make a quadrant. So he called his disciples to Himself and said unto them, Assuredly I say unto you that this poor widow has put in more than all those who have given to the treasury: For they all put in according to their abundance; but she out of her poverty put in all that she had, her whole livelihood. (Mark 12:41–44)*

Two mites equal a farthing. One farthing equals approximately .03¾ of a cent. Jesus said she gave *more* than the others. He was making a valuable ministry point: she gave all her living what she needed for food, clothing, and shelter. Instead she gave it to the Lord's work. Why?

In her heart, she decided God's needs were greater than her own. *Value is determined by the purpose of a gift.* The purpose of the widow's gift was twofold: the purpose for which it was given and the purpose in her heart of putting the work of God before her own need. Giving out of her need was a sacrifice.

The value of a gift is also determined by the sacrifice of the giver. A sacrifice is not made when we give our leftovers after we have had our fill. A sacrifice is made when we give to others something we need ourselves. We're giving out of our own need. This type of giving is multiplied back to the giver a hundredfold. The law of giving and receiving is the same for the Christians and non-Christians alike. The multiplication table is the same. What the difference is the non-Christian receives, but the receiving is not accompanied by God's anointing, thus leaving out peace and satisfaction that only God's anointing can bring.

In both stories, others were touched spiritually by the gifts given by the little girl and the widow. *The value of a gift is also determined by the lives touched by the gift.*

We're still touched today by this gift of the widow's mite.

The gifts the others gave were used for God's purpose but only touched the lives of that day and didn't last. Their gifts were used for the temple and the priests (much like today's gifts, which are used for the ministry of the church—the pastor's salary, new church pews, new sound system). In time, however, the value of the gifts depleted, but the value of the widow's mite is still being multiplied today, touching hearts and changing lives.

The Miracle of the Loaves

Let's look at another illustration the Lord gives us: the miracle of the loaves (John 6:5−13). Keep in mind that in order for something to be classified as a miracle, it has to have the hand of God on it, a supernatural intrusion. That is just what happens in this story.

> *"Then Jesus lifted up his eyes, and seen a great multitude coming toward him, he said to Philip, Where shall we buy bread, that these may eat? ... Philip answered Him, Two hundred denarii worth of bread is not sufficient for them, that every one of them may have a little" (John 6:5,7).*

Wrong thinking—*we don't have enough money in our treasury.* The Lord tells us that before we start a project, we are to take account of affordability. We have a tendency of carrying over those thoughts for decisions about what God can do into our ministries, churches, or homes by the amount of money we have. By doing so, we limit what God can do by the amount of available money we can see. At that point we are depending not upon God but our money.

The disciples looked to their treasury to supply the bread for the multitude. *Does God depend upon our money to determine what He can do spiritually, or do we depend upon God to supply the money He needs to complete the work He gave us to do?*

In my business I go into cities and countrysides alike and see small churches that are just trying to keep their doors open. They pray for enough to pay their current bills. People seem saddened by their plights. Across the street is a thriving ministry. That church is growing, ministering in the community, doing for the community, and people seem much happier. What's the difference? They are in the same town and same workforce, and they have the same industry, same opportunities, and same hardships. It doesn't make sense.

In my business I get to deal with many leaders of ministries of all sizes. What I find is this: (Keep in mind this isn't always the case; however, it is in the majority of times.) With stagnant churches, when an idea for ministry is presented, they immediately go to their treasurer to see if they can afford to do it. If the money isn't there, they won't undertake the ministry. I've heard many say, "If we have to borrow money, we aren't going to do it." That statement is fine when they are operating on faith but wrong when they are operating on fear.

They're depending upon their treasury to determine what God can do in their church. These churches have not gone anywhere, are not doing much ministry, and will never go anywhere, therefore remaining stagnant. They don't reach out to the community because they're too busy reaching out to their own needs. I know that is a bold statement to make, but just think about it.

If you're depending on your treasurer to determine what God can do in your church, you can never do anything more than one week. That is all your treasury will allow. Don't you have to come to church next week and put more money into the treasury? That's why they'll never grow beyond where they currently are. When they reach their goal of paying bills, they've accomplished what they set out to do and won't reach any further. They feel that if they have excess at the end of the month, if they use it for ministry other than bills, they won't have enough for the following month's expenses.

They get a feeling of accomplishment because they have ministered to themselves. They reject new ministry ideas because their faith will go no further than the treasury. They claim they're being good stewards. Good stewards of what? Of money or God's work? If their money is not being used for the work God wants them to do, they're not being good stewards. These are the churches that look at growing churches and offer reasons why those are growing and excuses for why they are not.

They measure value by their own standards. What about the growing churches? When a ministry idea is presented to them, they first go to their knees instead of looking at their treasury. Why? They seek God to see if it is His will. If it's determined that it is God's will, they move forward on God's promise instead of what they see in the treasury. They believe God will provide the funds to pay for it. *God never, never, never gives a vision that He does not equip and provide for its completion.* Spiritual decisions should never be made by the amount of money on hand. Instead, decisions should be made based on the anointing of God.

God honors those who have the faith! I can tell many stories of how God has provided when His people demonstrate faith. Those who lack that kind of faith say the faithful ones are in a better area where jobs are plentiful and rich people are around. These people actually believe that God needs a city, good jobs, and rich people to do His work. They have to see those things before they believe God will do it. They exercise faith in people and not God. Can they not see that it is our faith that God honors, not our location? If we can find the faith, God will find a way. We must first step out on faith. When we do that, God moves to provide the funds (not the opposite).

"One of his disciples, Andrew, Simon Peter's brother, said to Him,

There is a lad here, who has five barley loaves, and two small fishes: but what are they among so many" (John 6:8–9)?

Wrong thinking—*we don't have enough food.* They looked to their own food supply to provide. This is a natural response. After all, if you told your wife, "By the way, honey, I invited five thousand people to lunch today," what kind of a response would you get? At that point, I wouldn't want to be in your shoes. She may say that you barely have enough for yourselves. Naturally you'd check the cupboards and then make a trip to the grocery store for added company.

Now let's say Jesus told you to prepare a meal for five thousand, and you knew it was His directive. What would your response be? If Jesus gave you the command, then Jesus will take care of the food. The Lord has an unlimited expense account and always, always, always pays His bills.

Both individuals and churches struggle with determining what the church provides for its basic necessities and what directive Jesus gives us to follow. This is why it's so important that when a ministry idea is presented, the first place we should go is to our knees. Is it God's will? If our spirit bears witness that it is, even if we don't see it in the treasury, God will provide it. Too many people and churches take the easier route. It's much easier to say, "We can't afford it. The money isn't in the treasury."

How do you know for sure if it's the Lord's will? The first thing to do in determining His will is to ask, "Does it align with the Great Commission?" If it falls within the guidelines, does that mean this idea should be moved upon? Another determination to make is God's timing. We don't want to get behind the Lord, and we don't want to get ahead of Him. We want to be on the same page as Him. That needs to be determined by sincere prayer. A word of caution here: that determination should never be based on the money that's on hand or what we can see coming in; it should be made by determining if it is the anointing of God.

Let's get back to the story:

- They measured meals by their standards, not what Jesus could provide through faith.
- Jesus used what they had, not what they didn't have.
- The boy gave all his lunch, which was enough to supply himself with one meal (sacrifice).

This has always been confusing to me. Why is it that out of five thousand people, a young lad was the only one who had sense enough to bring his lunch? Could it be that Jesus knew ahead of time it would be needed and impressed upon the boy to bring it? Jesus never asks us to do something in ministry that He has not already provided for prior to the asking. If we all believed that, we wouldn't have a need to worry about.

> *"And Jesus said; Make the people sit down ... So the men sat down, in number about five thousand" (John 6:10).*

The number of people to be fed was immaterial. No matter how many were there, Jesus would have multiplied the necessary amount to meet that need.

> *"And Jesus took the loaves, and when He gave thanks, He distributed them to the disciples, and the disciples to those sitting down; and likewise of the fish as much as they wanted" (John 6:11).*

A child gave to Jesus for His purpose. The Lord doesn't get into arithmetic much, especially subtraction, but He sure can multiply! Notice that He didn't multiply anything except what was given. When the Lord blesses, He multiplies. The food was measured according to the need.

- Distribute as Jesus instructs, and the need will be filled.
- Smorgasbord style—eat all you want. No matter how much of the Bread of Life we eat, we can eat until we are full. It will not run out.

We can exhaust all our supplies. We can and will run out if we use it all for ourselves. Withholding from God will cause a shortage. However, what we give into the hands of Jesus He multiplies and multiplies. So as long as we continue to give to the Lord's work, we can never run out of supplies. Jesus says what we withhold from Him will be divided, and what we give will be multiplied.

Do you want your supplies, financial and otherwise, to be divided or multiplied? Hopefully your answer is multiplied. Then you have to do what multiplies, and that is give to Jesus. (Remember what Jesus said in Matthew 25:40: *"Inasmuch as ye have done it unto one of the least of these, my brethren, ye have done it unto me."*)

> *"So when they were filled, He said to His disciples, Gather up the fragments that remain, so that nothing is lost. Therefore they gathered them up, and filled twelve baskets with the fragments of the five barley loaves, which were left over by those who had eaten" (John 6:12–13).*

God used the gift to feed the five thousand, and the need was filled completely. God used the gift to feed the disciples, rewarding those who carried out His instructions. Incidentally the disciples did not understand what Jesus was telling them. They didn't know that as soon as the food left the basket, the basket would become full again. They just followed Jesus's instructions. This is why it's so important to follow Jesus without having to see where the road is going. God used the gift to feed the lad. The gift was returned to the giver, pressed down and running over.

Jesus in the Garden

This is one of the most touching stories in the Bible. It brings out the human nature of our Lord and offers spiritual victory in a situation the enemies of the Lord meant for defeat. When those of the world attempt to bring harm to God's children, our Lord is able to use that destructive situation and bring victory through it and use it as a blessing. This is a lesson we all can learn. There are things that happen in our lives that make it seem like the enemy is winning and we are facing defeat. Looking at the situation and judging from what we can physically see, it seems, on the surface, like sure defeat.

The late Tony Snow was a well-known newsman, former White House spokesperson, and a man of strong character who was well respected by his peers, family, and friends. He was known for his honesty and public profession as a Christian. When the news of his untimely death at the age of fifty-three came, it carried a positive context of admiration of this man, but it also dwelled on the fact that he had lost his battle with cancer. These reporters were looking at the physical nature of the sickness and the result. They reported with all good intentions, but they were giving the disease victory over his life. Nothing could be further from the truth.

The cancer did not defeat Tony Snow; Tony Snow defeated the cancer. He was tested and proven much stronger than the disease that attacked him. Through it all, he looked death and pain in the face and smiled with the confidence of knowing that no matter what the cancer did to his body, it could never destroy him. He knew with Jesus living in him, he could never die. I imagine in the quiet of his home he prayed the same prayer

Jesus prayed: "If this cup may not pass away from me, except I drink it, thy will be done" (Matt. 26:42).

> *"Knowing that he who raised up the Lord Jesus Christ will also raise us up with Jesus, and will present us with you. For all things are for your sakes, that grace, having spread through the many, may cause thanksgiving to abound to the glory of God. Therefore we do not lose heart. Even though our outward man is perishing, yet the inward man is being renewed day by day.*
>
> *For our light affliction, which is but for a moment, is working for us a far more exceeding and eternal weight of glory. While we do not look at the things which are seen, but at the things which are not seen. For the things which are seen are temporary, but the things which are not seen are eternal" (2 Cor. 4:14–18).*
>
> *"We are confident, yes, well pleased rather to be absent from the body, and to be present with the Lord" (2 Cor. 5:8).*

Did the cancer defeat Tony Snow, or did Tony Snow defeat the cancer? Did death on the cross defeat Jesus, or did Jesus defeat death? The answer to both those questions are the same: they defeated death. Jesus wasn't held on the cross by the nails; the nails were held by the hands of Jesus. The tomb didn't hold Jesus; Jesus shut Himself in the tomb. Hell couldn't hold Him; it had to release Him. The stone on the tomb didn't keep Jesus in; it kept the world out and moved out of the way to show the world He wasn't there. Walls couldn't keep Jesus out; they kept the disciples in. Gravity couldn't hold Jesus as He ascended to the Father. The world and those who declared Him an enemy couldn't destroy Him. They declared victory when they saw Him die, but when He resurrected they realized that it was they who had been defeated. Yes, Jesus swallowed death in victory. When you follow Jesus, never believe what you see. See what you believe.

> *"And He took with Him Peter and the two sons of Zebedee, and He began to be very sorrowful and deeply distressed" (Matt. 26:37).*

God asked more of those closest to Him. If you are close to Jesus, more will be required of you. When you are by his side, you are within His reach and the sound of His voice. The closer you get to Him, the better you hear him. *"Draw nigh to God, and he will draw nigh to you" (James 4:8).*

> *"Then He said to them, My soul is exceeding sorrowful, even to death: stay here and watch with me" (Matt. 26:38).*

The sacrifice He was about to make meant a lot to Him. He had to give up something which was most valuable: His own life. It wasn't easy for Jesus to give up His life. He felt what we feel. He could have called it off at any moment. He could have called ten thousand angels, but instead He died for you and me.

> *"He went a little farther, and fell on His face, and prayed, saying, O my Father, if it were possible, let this cup pass from me; nevertheless, not as I will, but as You will" (Matt. 26:39).*

Not looking forward to the pain, He knew He would suffer by giving this gift. *Nevertheless, not as I will but as God will.* The Lord asks us to give out of our need and not what is unwanted or left over. We are to give our best for the Master. Jesus gave His best: His life. I really need this gift for myself, but

- I trust you with it;

- You know best, God;
- You and Your work are more important than my life.

What is the value of Jesus's gift? What are the results?

1. Without it we could not be saved.
2. Two thousand years of changed lives.
3. Millions and millions receive eternal life.
4. God gave His only Son.

One gift used for God's purpose has brought value to the human race that cannot be measured by man's scale and is still multiplying to this day.

What is Your Gift Worth?

Do you sacrifice from what you need or give what is left over after you are full? If the little boy had done that, nobody would have eaten but the boy. Do you trust God to do the right thing with your gift? Is it used for His purpose? Do you believe God can multiply it back to you?

When it comes to giving, the worst thing you can do is compare your giving with others and feel complacent because you're giving as much or more than they are. I have to admit, I fell into that trap. I asked myself the question, "Should I give more?" I compared my giving to the giving of others in the congregation. We would get an annual report that showed our percent of giving to the rest of the church. As long as I was in the upper 3 to 5 percent, I felt I didn't need to give more. That was the worst mistake I could make. God let me know my error. We should never compare our giving to others or let them decide if we should give more or less. Instead, compare your gift in relation to what God has given you.

Don't ever feel that your gift is too small for the Lord to

use, that it is insignificant and can't do much. Remember the widow's mite. Don't ever feel that you're giving enough or too much. You cannot outgive God. *"Give, and it will be given to you: good measure, pressed down, shaken together, and running over"* *(Luke 6:38).*

How can you lose by giving to God? There is no gift too small or too big for God to multiply. Your dollar could change the lives of thousands and also your own. Remember the next time you give that Jesus is standing by the treasury of your heart and watching for purpose of the gift: resentment, personal glory, pride, doubt, sacrifice, faith, or love. He will value your gift according to the purpose in your heart and according to the sacrifice made. Keep on giving until God stops giving to you.

Chapter 11 Action Project

I will do the following:

1. Not compare my giving to someone else but instead compare my giving to that which God has blessed me.
2. Start to stretch my giving. I will stretch it to what my own faith allows. Then in thirty days, I will stretch it some more and continue to stretch it every thirty days. I realize that no matter how far I stretch it, I cannot break it.
3. Recognize that when I give, Jesus is evaluating the treasure of my heart to see the purpose of my gift. Is it given grudgingly, out of necessity, or out of love?
4. Give not out of my excess but out of my need.

Chapter 12: God's Bank

WE have come a long way in transforming our thinking from worldly to godly. All of our actions are conceived in the mind, and our minds transform thoughts into actions. That is when it becomes a reality in our lives. Hopefully you are putting into practice what you have learned or perhaps what you already knew and needed reassurance on.

The important thing is you have learned how to prosper and there is nothing on, in, or around the earth that can stop God from making His prosperity a reality in your life. You have also learned that no matter what the enemy does, he cannot destroy, distort, or ruin a life that is dedicated to the Lord Jesus. It may seem like this is the end, but it is only the beginning. What lies ahead of you in your years of prosperity on this earth is minor compared to what God has in store for you in heaven. It is so great that Paul could not even find words to explain it. As great as it is being a child of God, you should know what lies ahead.

I'm sure you've heard someone say they'll wait until later to make a decision for the Lord. First, God may not give them that chance later when He is calling today; however, what they don't realize is that when they get to heaven, they will receive rewards according to their works on earth. The word *works* isn't a dirty word. I've spoken to people so adamant about it that they don't do anything for the Lord because they don't want anyone to think they're working their way to heaven. We have to put that word in the proper context. According to God's Word, this is it in a nutshell:

We don't do good works to get saved; we do good works because we are saved.

As we begin this last chapter, we know the Lord doesn't offer much Scripture describing heaven. Most of the biblical descriptions tell us what's not there rather than what's there. That alone is enough excitement to want to spend eternity there. Let's look at what is not there:

> *"And God will wipe away all tears from their eyes. And there will be no more death, nor mourning, nor crying out, nor will there be any more pain; for the first things passed away" (Rev 21:4).*

1. **If there are no tears, there must be no sorrow.**

- If there is no sorrow, there must be only perfect love and perfect happiness.
- If there is eternal happiness, there cannot be losses of any kind.
- We must have all our needs supplied, and I believe there will be some type of works for us to do. Whatever it is, we will always have the means to do them without having to have a special offering or lack of funds of any kind.
- If our needs are supplied, there can be no want for anything. Translated, we will have everything we need or ever dreamed of needing.

2. **If there is no death nor mourning,**

- there must be only life.

3. **If there is no crying out,**

- there can be no more heartaches or sorrows, and
- there can be no worry or anxiety or discomfort of any kind.

4. **If there will be no more pain,**

- there cannot be accidents, bleeding, heart attacks, cancer, or any other of the life-threatening diseases, and
- if there cannot be any of these, we must have a body created by the hand of God that is suitable for eternal existence. One that would be recognizable by your loved ones here on earth yet perfect in every sense of the word.

5. **If first things are passed away and all things become new,**

- when something is new it is at its best. The newness will remain for eternity and will never change. It will remain new for eternity.

Wow, who can ask for anything more? But there is more. Please read on.

Let's take some of the Scripture as it relates to this study. Let's look at heaven as not only the throne of God but also as a place like the Federal Reserve here in the United States a place where God stores all our good deeds and what we have given to God and others in need. It is heaven's bank.

Ask yourself this question: *When I die and go to be with the Lord, what can I take with me?* The immediate answer may be, "Nothing!" God tells us in the book of Job, "Naked came I out of my mother's womb, and naked I shall return thither" (Job

1:21). What God was referring to are the material things on this earth what we can see, taste, touch, or smell. It's pointless to spend our lives laying up material items we cannot take with us. This lesson points out that we can take it with us, referring to spiritual things. The only thing we can take with us is what we give.

> *"Assuredly I say unto you, whatever you bind on earth will be bound in heaven: and whatever you loose on earth will be loosed in heaven" (Matt. 18:18).*

Salvation is a gift of God. We are saved by grace and not by works; however, our works on earth have a definite bearing on what we will receive in heaven. We do have control over what we will receive in relation to what we sow on earth. James says *"Without works faith is dead"* (2:20).

What we do for self soon will pass; only what we do for God will last. Take a minute to think about this. Everything we do for self in this world will pass; however, everything we do for God will last, not just in this lifetime but in our heavenly home the little things you do for others, the work of the church, things nobody ever sees. But God does see, and the good you do will be rewarded here and in heaven. Being seen by man is not important, but doing for the Lord is. Our deeds, large and small, do not escape the watchful eye of our Lord. His eyes are what counts, regardless of what others see. God not only prospers us with blessings in doing His will on this earth, but He also blesses us with heavenly riches when we leave this earth.

> *"For the Son of man will come in the glory of his Father with his angels; and then He will reward each according to his works" (Matt. 16:27).*

If man is rewarded according to his work, what work? It has to be spiritual. We will take with us only what we give to God. God is not speaking of salvation because that is not of our works but His grace. He is speaking of our ministry to others and for others and our obedience to His voice.

Not too long ago I was at an awards banquet at which the leaders of the company were to receive bonus checks. One of the gentlemen discussed with me the advantages and disadvantages of investing in land or the stock market. He was paying high taxes, and the taxes were going to take most of his bonus. He asked me where I put mine to get the most for my money. It didn't take me long to answer that question. "We just give more," I said.

When I think of what the Lord has done for Laverne and me through our giving and how He has multiplied our income, there is not an investment on earth that would compare. We have found that our number-one investment is in the Kingdom. How do you explain that?

God's Bank

What comes to our minds when we think of banks?

- Safety of principal and interest
- Place of security where money won't be stolen or burned
- Guaranteed
- Good service
- Convenience
- Money there when you need it

You don't drown by falling into water. You drown by staying there. Trouble can get us down, but we don't have to invite it to stay. Its only purpose is to discourage us and make us miserable. What seems to cause us the most worry is finances. Will we lose or gain? We can really develop some financial woes in our bookkeeping. We need to pray and then pick ourselves up by our bootstraps and move on. Jesus can walk with us only when we move in faith toward the answer to our prayer.

Never try to save out of God's cause; such money will canker (make useless) the rest. Giving to God is no loss; it is a deposit into God's bank. Giving is true having, as the old gravestone said. Remember this true little verse from past lessons:

What I spent I had.

What you spent is gone; you'll never see it again.

What I saved I lost.

What you saved will stay behind; again, you'll never see it again.

What I gave I have.

What you gave can never be taken away from you.

You can never lose it, and it doesn't stay behind; it goes with you, or should I say it went on ahead of you. Most of the world's troubles are produced by those who don't produce anything else. How true this is. If you think about it, who produces the world's troubles? Yes, the idle mind that does not produce anything else. Those with bankrupt minds can think of nothing but causing trouble. That's the only thing they can do well. If you could look into the window of their souls like Jesus does, you can see people who don't like themselves and are unhappy with what they see.

Review of Some Facts

Not giving is hording. Hording is always caused by fear. Remember, fear and doubt are traveling companions. Christians operate by faith.

There are no problems financial or otherwise that are impossible for God. If we know this, why do we go about as if we have unique needs or problems that are too big for God?

There is no shortage of money in God's church, only a shortage of faithful people. O my, did that hurt! I am sorry to say it; nonetheless, it is true. The best place for Christians to look for funds to meet the obligations of the church is their own pockets. If we really believed that we cannot outgive God, then there would be no shortage of funds in the church.

Think about the time when Jesus and Peter were entering Capernaum and there were those collecting tribute. They asked Peter if his master paid tribute, and Peter said yes. Jesus railed on Peter for telling him that. But listen to what Jesus told Peter to do:

"Nevertheless, lest we offend them, go to the sea, cast in a hook, and take the fish that comes up first. And when you have opened his mouth, you will find a piece of money; take that and give it to them for Me and you" (Matt. 17:27). If Jesus can cause a fish to pay tribute, how much more will He create or lead us to? Enough funds to take care of us and our families? Our part is not to be able to see how Jesus will provide or where it will come from but rather to have faith that He will provide.

The example that you set in giving will cause others to give. We have a natural tendency to claim that for which we work as "ours" and not God's. If we have that mindset, we'll always put our needs before God's. We'll also always be in want and never have peace with our finances.

God wants to bless His children and share His wealth. God created wealth for His children. When His children are found unfaithful, He gives it to the wicked. Think again the next time you find yourself asking why the wicked have so much more. The answer is because God's people have been searched and found unfaithful. The unfaithful would rather give it to the wicked instead of God's children even though they know it will be used for ill gain against the Christian causes.

Seek out Christians to give to those in need and do business with them, giving to the Kingdom. How could we ever love the world enough to evangelize it if we refuse to take care of our own?

Prosperity isn't automatic because we are Christians. We must follow the instructions God wrote in the book for us. It is called putting feet on our prayers. If you trust in your riches, you forget God, rebellion sets in, and you deny Him in your actions.

> *"And again I say to you, It is easier for a camel to go through the eye of a needle, than for a rich man to enter the kingdom of God" (Matt. 19:24).*

Then Jesus qualified that statement: *"But Jesus looked at them, and said to them, With men this is impossible, but with God all things are possible" (Matt. 19:26).*

- God wants his children to prosper.
- He teaches us to do His will.
- True satisfaction can only come internally, not externally.
- Prosperity of fools shall destroy them.

When we see those who lie, cheat, and steal get ahead and seem to prosper, we need to keep in mind that we really don't want to be in their shoes. Their very prosperity, for which they lied, cheated, and stole, will destroy them. On the other hand, the prosperity of the righteous shall magnify them. If you had a choice either to live in a mansion and be miserable or live in a shack and be happy, which would you select? I'm not saying that by choosing God's prosperity you'll live in a shack. This is just an illustration. Money can buy a lot of things but not happiness. When you're in God's will, you are happy, and when you're happy, you'll enjoy your money regardless of the amount, large or small. God's Word allows us to enjoy prosperity without sorrow.

The last time you failed, did you stop trying because you failed, or did you fail because you stopped trying? There is an old saying in the insurance business: winners never quit, and quitters never win. When you try hard unsuccessfully, when defeat seems eminent and you just feel like quitting, *pray for a second breath*. If you quit at that point, you are defeated, and you were defeated because you quit. *The only time you can ever fail is when you quit or blame your defeat on something or somebody else.* If you continue on even if victory is not on the horizon, you can never fail. We need to place ourselves in a position to be blessed by God.

Making Deposits in God's Bank

What happens when you make a deposit in your hometown bank?

- You transfer funds from your pocket into an account with your name on it to be used at a future date. Funds in the bank accumulate interest.
- You don't lose the money; you just transfer it.
- This is profitable for the bank because they have the use of it.
- You'll use it at a future date when you need it most.
- You'll have more because interest accumulates on the amount you deposited.

What happens when you give to God?

- You transfer it from your pocket into God's bank account in your own name.
- You don't lose it; you transfer it from one hand to the other.

253

- It will collect interest.
- The Lord gets to use it for His cause right now.
- You'll use it at a future date when you need it most on earth and in heaven.
- You get it back with interest.

God always gives back what we give, pressed down, shaken together, and running over.

> *"And the King will answer and say to them, Assuredly I say to you, Inasmuch as you did it to one of the least of these My brethren, you did it to me" (Matt. 25:40).*

- What we do for others in the form of meeting a need, helping, aiding, or giving, we are doing to God Himself, especially to those of the household of faith.
- The "least of these" are the most needy.
- Sometimes it may seem that those you help don't appreciate it or are just taking advantage of you. Keep in mind you're not giving to them only; you are giving to God. Those to whom we give must answer to God, as we do. We can't make them do the right thing, but we can make sure we do the right thing in God's eyes.

> *"Do not lay up treasures on earth for yourselves, where moth and rust corrupt, and where thieves break through and steal. But lay up treasures in Heaven for yourselves, where neither moth nor rust corrupt, and where thieves do not break through nor steal. For where your treasure is, there will your heart be also" (Matt. 6:19–21).*

- **What treasure?** That which carries a value.
- **How is it laid up?** It's put aside, saved.
- **Who is it for?** Yourself. You care for yourself by

caring for the needs of others. You also get a benefit from it.

- **Where is it kept**? In heaven. If doing unto the least of these is doing unto God, then He takes your deeds and our gifts and places them in heaven. So it's not a loss to us but a savings.
- **Why?** To keep it safe and you worry free.

Your heart will be where your treasure is. It all comes down to where your heart is. That's where you'll put your treasure. What is the closest thing to your heart? When we take that which is of value to us and give it for the good of others, we're meeting a need for God's purpose. He places our gift in an account in heaven with our names on it. That is our heavenly bank account.

Placing Money in Christ's Hand

A pastor was taking a missionary collection when he said, "I want each of you to give today as though you were putting your money right into the pierced hand of Jesus Christ."

Afterward a lady came up to him said, "I was going to give a half dollar, but I didn't."

"Why not?" the preacher asked.

"Do you think I would put a half dollar into His pierced hand? I have ten dollars at home, and I am going to give that."

If we were putting our money into the pierced hand of our Lord, our contributions would amount to millions, and the world would be evangelized in ten years (author unknown).

If you treat a person as he or she is, he or she will remain as he or she is. If you treat him or her for what he or she could be, he or she will become what he or she could be. I made this statement in a group of ministers. One spoke up and said, "Not necessarily so." He was responding from experience. If someone is lazy and doesn't want to be helped, no matter how you treat him or her, he or she will amount to nothing.

Let me qualify that statement: If you have someone who isn't lazy and truly wants to do well, you cannot make him or her better by pointing out his or her faults and putting him or her down. Doing so will drive that person down, and he or she will have low self-esteem. On the other hand, if you treat that person like you know he or she can be, he or she will become what he or she could be. Isn't that the way Jesus treats us?

How Do You Open an Account in Heaven?

When you present yourself to the Lord, ask forgiveness for your sin, and ask Jesus to come into your heart, you are opening a bank account in heaven. Your father, mother, sister, brother, friend, or minister cannot open it for you. You must make the decision yourself. This is a decision you make alone, but you need not travel alone after that decision. You have the Lord within you. He promises to walk with you. You have Christian friends to encourage you, the Holy Spirit to teach you, faith to strengthen you, and a vision to inspire you.

The majority of non-Christians don't realize that even though they have people around with like habits and failures, they are misguided into thinking they are not alone. Nothing can be further from the truth. A person without Christ is a very lonely person. You see, the road of sadness, misery, and heartache is also a road you must travel alone. Christians, however, make the decision alone to follow Christ, and from that time forward they will never, ever be alone.

Every time we give to God's cause our time, service, talent, energy, or money we are making a deposit in that account. When we give money, we are making a withdrawal from our checking account on earth and placing it in the hands of God, and He deposits it in our heavenly account. When we write a check, we don't lose the money; it is transferred to God's bank in our name.

- The transfer is made in faith.
- God invests our deposit in the best possible place, where it will bear the highest interest, giving us the greatest return.
- God's bank is not the stock exchange; therefore, it's not subject to fluctuation of market conditions.
- Our investment is not affected by a recession or depression.
- It's not subject to unemployment losses.
- God doesn't deduct any taxes from it.
- Our politicians can't reach it.
- It is fully insured, with no limits.
- Interest is always high.
- Principle is guaranteed for eternity.
- Its value is never depleted by economic conditions.
- It can't be stolen or burned.

I could give, but I could not see how. I did give and the Lord helped me. I have had some work, my garden grows well, and never since have I stopped to think twice when I have heard of some needy one. No, if I gave away all, the Lord would not let me stray. It is like money in the bank, only this time the bank never breaks, and the interest comes back every day (*Log of the Good Ship Grace*).

We Cannot Transfer It to Someone Else

While reading earlier chapters, were you asking yourself, "If God owns all the silver and gold, why He just doesn't give it to us because we ask for it?" Now you know. I'm sure if it were possible, every Christian would want to open an account for their whole family, knowing they have unsaved loved ones who are lost and don't know it. We know if something happens to them, they will not be going to heaven because of their unbelief. We love them so much that we just wish we could make that decision for them.

However, salvation is not joining a church, completing a class, or being born into a certain nationality or religion. It is believing in Jesus Christ, God's only Son, who gave His life on the cross, shed His blood for the forgiveness of sin, entered into the tomb, and rose the third day. The truth is we cannot be saved as a family, class, or group. It is an individual decision to follow Jesus. I would just love to open an account for many of my family members, but I cannot, and neither can you. They must open their own accounts. We cannot save anyone; only Jesus can save. Jesus said, "I am the way, the truth, and the life: no man can cometh unto the Father, but by me" (John 14:6).

Only responsible people have the capability of love. Jesus teaches us how to love how to do for others and not just for ourselves. He teaches us to look out for each other and not just ourselves. God is a loving God and wants us to follow Him because we love Him. God knows that if He gives everything we want when we ask for it, when we demand it, when we feel we are entitled to it, eventually we will spend our eternity in the eternal lake of fire.

Each person has to open his or her own account in heaven. Each person has to make his or her own deposits. Each person will receive interest in direct proportion to what he or she deposits, which is the highest in the universe. When we deposit in God's bank, all of our needs will be met, and we'll have plenty left over.

Faith Without Works Is Like an Automobile Without Gas

At this very hour, the most brilliant minds in the world are trying to make an automobile that runs without gas. They read about it; they talk and have meetings about it. From their talking, they decide which way is the best way to go, and then they move toward developing such an automobile. Now, if they stopped at talking about it, nothing would ever get developed.

That is the way it is with prayer. Prayer is a two-way communication with God. We ask him directions; He points us in the right direction; and we get up and go to work. Why would we think that we would just get everything by talking to God? It is when we get up from our knees in prayer that we need to move on our prayers in faith. God calls us to walk in faith, not sit in faith.

The Challenge

1. Bloom where you are planted. Start from where you are right now.
2. Increase your giving by 10 to 15 percent.
3. Increase your giving at the beginning of each month.
4. Stretch your giving. No matter how far you stretch it, you cannot break it.
5. Then stretch it a little further every month.

Exercising our faith makes it stronger, not weaker. When we exercise our bodies, we exercise the area that needs strength. If we want to build up our arms, we exercise our arms. We get weights or barbells to do so. It is not until our muscles meet resistance that they grow. The more resistance they meet, the stronger they grow. We start out with small weights until our bodies get used to it. The more we exercise, the easier it becomes. We then add on a little more weight until we can handle the extra.

There's a story of a gentleman who got a calf and lifted him every day. As the calf grew, the man became stronger. Lifting every day, he didn't notice the increase in size of the cow. The cow and his muscles were growing at the same time. So it is with increasing our faith in giving. We can't grow in faith until we meet some resistance. So we have to get off center if we're going to grow. Our center could be what we are sitting on or resting our excuses on. We expand our giving according to what our faith will allow. You may wish to give an extra dollar a week while others may increase at five or ten dollars per week. As we become accustomed to that type of giving, our faith will increase. We then give that much again the second month, and our faith grows more. We can continue that for the rest of our lives, and we will never break our faith. The more we give, the stronger our faith becomes. The more we give, the more the Father gives us. Being that we cannot outgive God, the only time God will stop increasing His giving to us is when we stop exercising our faith. We set the limit. God doesn't.

God will continue increasing until the day we die if we continue to grow our faith. When you place God before your money, you're placing yourself in a position for God to pour out blessings you won't have room to receive. Don't stop until God stops blessing you.

Summary

We've gone over a lot of Scripture but have only scratched the surface. We've addressed many reasons or excuses why we don't give. However, there are only two real reasons why we don't give to God:

1. We do not believe Him.

2. We don't trust Him.

It's up to you to take the information in this book and use it for your future prosperity for your family, your church, your God, and yourself. What are you going to do with that knowledge? It's in your hands.

Shack in Heaven

In his short story "The Mansion," Henry van Dyke tells of a wealthy businessman who considered himself a Christian but would give only to causes that would yield him a good return for his investment. One night after an argument with his son, he fell asleep and dreamed he went to heaven. The Keeper of the Gate took him on a tour. As they walked past unbelievable mansions, the businessman said he lived in the best mansions on earth, but nothing could compare with these, with such beauty as far as the eye could see.

Finally they came to a broken down shack. The Keeper of the Gate told him, "This is your mansion."

The businessman was taken back. "There must be some mistake," he said.

"There is no mistake," said the Keeper of the Gate very calmly. "Here is your name, the record of your title, and your possessions in this place."

"But how could such a house be prepared for me … for me, after my long and faithful service? Is this a suitable mansion for one so well-known and devoted? Why is it so pitifully small and mean? Why have you not built it large and fair like the others?"

"That is all the material you sent us."

I encourage you to go from this place and look for people in need and places to give of your time, talent, and energy, and you will experience wealth beyond measure. By applying the principles laid out in Scripture and proved by man, you will see prosperity come into your life like you never dreamed possible.

By all Christians doing the same, you will see a transfer of wealth from the wicked to the faithful. In so doing, the church will reclaim that which God intended for His children.

Giving your wealth to save the wicked does not increase the wicked but increases the Kingdom. Giving to other Christian works and doing business with Christians enriches the Kingdom. I encourage searching out Christian businessmen to do business with. God left the choice to you which one you will increase. Keep in mind that when you patronize non–Christian businessmen, you are supporting the places they give their money, and I assure you, it isn't the church.

> *"Choose forever yourselves this day whom ye will serve ... but as for me and my house, we will serve the LORD" (Josh. 24:15).*

Make your decision for Christ today. Follow Him and obey His instructions, and the prosperity written about in this book is yours. The choice is yours. Open your hands toward heaven and give according to God's leading and prosper, or close your hand to withhold. Giving multiplies Kingdom works and your own prosperity. Withholding hinders work of the Kingdom and divides what you have.

- **Giving is not an obligation, it's an opportunity.**
- **It's more blessed to give than to receive.**
- **Giving is fun.**
- **Giving is our way of thanking God.**
- **Giving is our way of serving God.**
- **Giving is our way of trusting God.**
- **Giving is our way of pleasing God.**
- **Giving is our way of believing God.**
- **Giving is fruitful.**
- **Giving feels good.**
- **Giving is exciting.**

- **Give and it shall be given—pressed down and running over.**
- **Believe it.**
- **Do it.**
- **You cannot outgive God.**
- **May God enrich you with wealth, health, and happiness.**

Chapter 12 Action Project

From now and for the rest of my life, I will recognize the following:

1. I cannot outgive God.
2. Every time I meet the needs of another, I am making a deposit in God's bank account.
3. Giving is not a loss but a gain.
4. God always gives us back more than what we give.
5. When I die, I will take nothing physical out of this world.
6. When I die, the only thing I can take with me is what I gave away.

Appendix

Testimonies

AFTER I completed the study, I looked for an outlet to teach. I went to my own pastor for the opportunity. There was a room open in the youth wing during the Sunday school hour. I sent letters to those who didn't attend a Sunday school class, inviting them to attend the class for thirteen weeks. Thirty-four came to the first class, and we maintained twenty-eight throughout the entire course. It was made up of diverse walks of life. Because of the nature of the subject matter, I was pleased that we kept the students throughout the entire study.

During the class, two received the Lord into their lives. The students came out of the course looking for ways to get involved in ministry of the church and opportunities to give. Five months after the class, I asked the church treasurer to compare the percent of giving of the class members for the five-month period before the course to the five-month period after the class. My goal was a 20- to 25-percent increase in giving, but I would have settled for 10 to 15 percent.

The treasurer stopped me in the foyer one Sunday morning with excitement in his voice. He told me that there was a 76 percent increase in the five months after the class, which translated into $7,800 more. I had received a confirmation from the Lord that this is a study that every Christian truly needs.

—James Hooks

★ ★ ★

This is an important topic for Christians. It is a subject that most people get nervous about. We don't want to talk about money. In this class I learned Scriptures about money and where it should rank in my life. God's Word gives concrete answers to questions on balancing money, spending, giving, etc.

A statement was made in class: "Where faith in God is present, there can be no fear or doubt." I know God will lead and direct me in every aspect of my life, including finances. I have also learned that a prosperous person sees the needs of others and helps them to achieve their goals. I also realize that everything comes from God and we serve Him by ministering to the world. I am prosperous to have the blessings of friends and family. As quoted in our class, "It's not what you have; it's what you do with what you have that makes all the difference." I hope to make a difference.

—Charlene Magolis

★ ★ ★

Rich and I truly changed our lifestyle while attending the class on *Should Christians Prosper*. We learned that in our marriage we needed to set some boundaries and prioritize our finances. Bible verses and accounts were incorporated and explained to compare our present-day living arrangements. About halfway through the thirteen-week study, Rich and I made some changes. We put God in control of everything, including our finances. Budgeting excuses we had made before this study were overturned with explanations of tithing correctly and putting God first in everything.

We have honestly been blessed since we made the changes that we did because of attending this class together. We both still speak highly of the study and would definitely promote it to others, especially those who are struggling with their finances.

Sincerely,

Amy L. Smith

★ ★ ★

I just wanted to tell you how much I enjoyed and appreciated being in your class. It was such an inspiration and help to me. I gained and prospered from your class. Jim, you brought the lessons out so clear and easy to understand. I will miss your class.

—Laverne Nulf

★ ★ ★

It was not a coincidence being in your class. God had a purpose for my life. I was praying for help with my finances and asked God for a way out of debt. The Lord placed upon my heart to make a nurse's scrub that folds into its own pocket. I brought it to class to ask my teacher, Jim Hooks, for advice in marketing. He and God made me realize that I needed to make God first in my life by surrendering my life to Him, and Jim led me in the prayer of salvation. A few days later I was baptized. Since then my life has changed so much. I had followed God's Word and gave Him the first fruit. My shirts are selling slowly, but that's good. I have learned to love life more and appreciate how Jesus died for me. My future plans are to become a missionary so I can tell people of the wonderful Word of God and the great things He has done for me and will do the same for them.

Thank you, God, for everything.

Barb Pikins

★ ★ ★

Prior to preparing my testimony on the benefits of the study *Should Christians Prosper,* I reviewed my notebook, which was given to all in the class, and wow, what a reminder! The review took me back a few steps, and I was once again astonished as to how quickly we can lose focus when it comes to critical parts of our lives. I was reminded once again that this class influenced major decisions that were taking place, not only in my personal life but also in our business lives. The phrase "we will never outgive God" is a constant reminder in my day-to-day life. You will definitely find out that if you put your total trust, faith, and your pocketbook in God's hands, you will be rewarded.

I am grateful for the opportunity to share this and truly say once again what a blessing I received at a time in my life when I was asking, "Why me, Lord?" The class made me realize that we must truly give from the heart, and God will see us through all trials and tribulations which come our way. Thanks for the opportunity.

Yours truly,
Jess Miller

★ ★ ★

Dear Jim,

Even though as a Christian and a pastor I have always given over 10 percent, plus extra giving to special events as well as helping others, this conference challenged me to stretch even more and really trust God as never before. My wife and I started doing that, and it is amazing how God moved in special ways financially in our lives, plus I have a new perspective on giving that I did not have before. This conference has really helped our congregation. Giving is up, and folks are excited to stretch and see God work. He has in many of the folks who took the challenge. It is one of the best conferences I have seen in a long time. I would highly recommend it to anyone.

—Pastor Gary Bates

★ ★ ★

Dear Jim and Laverne,

We can't thank the Lord enough for opening the door for you to come and share your conference with us; it has helped us so tremendously. The answers to prayer and how God is working with the people here in their finances is awesome. Some got better jobs, some were able to get a newer car that they needed, others are seeing their money stretch further. Through His blessings our church was able to give me more personally and still save the church money at the same time. God is working in so many ways and we sure needed it!

God bless you both.

—Gary Bates

Hammer Street Church of God, Portage, Pa.

★ ★ ★

This study was excellent for Christians who struggle with the pros and cons of giving tithes and offerings. This study verified and clarified what I learned as a young Christian; that is, through difficult as well as good financial times, God will cause us to prosper beyond what we can imagine and in ways that are hard to believe. If we are faithful in giving willingly and generously, we can overcome, with the help of the Holy Spirit, one of Satan's biggest roadblocks to becoming a sanctified Christian.

—John R. Marley

Retired School Superintendent

★ ★ ★

My husband, Alvin, and I recently completed *Should Christians Prosper,* a study on biblical finance taught by Jim Hooks, a leader in our church. From time to time, we have felt our giving challenged even though the tithe had been our standard of measure as a couple since Alvin became a Christian in 1972. We often responded to special needs announced in the church. Through this study we felt stretched to give and then be stretched again.

We don't know how far God may take us, but to date we have increased our "regular" tithe, began a monthly support of a Para-church ministry, and doubled our Sunday school giving. One of our greatest blessings is the increased awareness of the needs of others and our joy to respond in some financial way to help meet it.

We expect our reward to be in heaven, although God is blessing us now with a few dollars left in our checking account at the end of the month, and He blesses us with good health while we both live with a chronic illness. We want to cultivate generosity in our lives and follow God's instructions to trust Him for those things we need and more to give away.

—Alvin and Dorothy Kendall

★ ★ ★

We had a financial mountain that we were trying to get around, through, over, or dig under for three years. Have you ever had more month at the end of the money? We have been there. The problem was *we were trying to control* our mountain. Matthew 17:20 says, "I tell you the truth, if you have faith as small as a mustard seed, you can say to this mountain, 'Move from here to there' and it will move. Nothing will be impossible for you."

This past winter, we attended Jim Hooks's class and we had the light bulb moment. We were sitting in Jim's class and both heard what he had to say. We made eye contact and knew what we needed to do; we were not tithing. See, we had been forgetting to look at our mountain from God's perspective.

Yes, we were giving an offering to the church, but we were not tithing. We said that we would begin tithing after we got this bill paid off or after this was done and so on. We were not giving the Lord what was His, not being good stewards of His money. He could not bless us because we were not doing what we should be doing.

So on Sunday, we wrote out our first tithe check. What a week we had! We had finally had a savings account, and on Monday my car needed repair work that cost almost four hundred dollars. On Tuesday, the kitchen sink clogged up; on Wednesday, the furnace quit working; and on Thursday, I had a wipeout in my car coming home from Punxsutawney, PA. But we wrote our check out again the next week. We told the Lord that He could have our savings account because it all belonged to Him anyway, and we have been receiving the blessings ever since. And the blessings continue in countless ways.

We are still being tested in many different ways, but it feels good to know that God is in control and that our mountain has been moved. What an awesome God we serve! (Matthew 17:20).

God is good, and He is the one thing that we can *always* count on to stick to His promises.

—Barry and Michelle Stahlman

★ ★ ★

I'd like to say that the information I received from your course has been such a blessing and has been so pivotal in my life. It's been life changing. It's because I took it to heart and have been changing the way I think. Okay, so here are a few things that have happened since class:

- I increased my giving. I did something really crazy, like give 30 percent initially! I had never done that before, and it was awesome! Several times I even gave 50 percent of my income.
- I had been praying for a new computer that could handle the work I was about to endeavor. So a few weeks ago, I got it!
- In early February, I prayed that God intervene and

make changes at my husband's job. A change needed to be made! Well, a few days later, the CEO of our local YMCA (a strong Christian man, who had developed a relationship with my husband over the past year) asked him to apply for the Director of Marketing position. Long story short, he got the position.

The great thing is God's been just blessing us one thing after the other. It's like this whole thing has just opened a floodgate of "doors" that I know would not have been opened had I not taken this course and got my mind right. God knows I've been so ready to just step out and go to the next level but just didn't quite know how. Your course helped to bring things full circle for me.

—Marla Parker

References and Suggested Reading

References

- **Ralph Waldo Emerson**
- **New King James**
- **Gospel Herald**
- **Sunday School Times**
- **Choice Gleanings Calendar**
- **Religious Telescope**
- **Shepard, Kohut, & Sweet**
- **Ellison research in Phoenix**
- **Log of the Good Ship Grace**

Suggested Reading

- *Trust God for Your Finances* by Jack Hartman *The Generosity Factor* by Ken J. Blanchard and S. Truett Cathy
- *The Blessed Life* by Robert Morris

About the Author

JAMES H. Hooks is a student of human condition, using God's Word to bring about positive life-changing experiences in our everyday battles with our faith and finances. A life changing balance was brought on, not by changing vocation but a change of thinking and a change of heart. A change from using the strength of others and the world to meet his needs, to use the strength of the Lord working through himself to meet the needs of others and the world needs. If was a transition that inspired the writing of this book Should Christians Prosper. He wants readers to not just read about his transition but experience it in their own lives.